Occult Fiction of Dion Fortune

The Occult Fiction of Dion Fortune

Gareth Knight

THOTH PUBLICATIONS
Loughborough, Leicestershire

Copyright 2007 Gareth Knight

All rights reserved. No reproduction, copy or transmission
of this publication may be made without written permission.
No paragraph of this publication may be reproduced, copied
or transmitted save with the written permission
or in accordance with the provision of the
Copyright Act 1956 (as amended).
Any person who does any unauthorised act in relation to this
publication may be liable for criminal prosecution
and civil claims for damages.

The Moral Rights of the Author have been asserted.

A CIP catalogue record for this book is available
from the British Library.

Cover design by Helen Surman

ISBN 978-1-870450-86-7

Printed and bound in Great Britain

Published by Thoth Publications
64, Leopold Street, Loughborough, LE11 5DN

Web address: www.thoth.co.uk
email: enquiries@thoth.co.uk

Contents

Part One
At The Portal Of The Mysteries

The Secrets Of Dr. Taverner.	11
The Demon Lover.	32

Part Two
The Mysteries Of Sun And Earth

The Winged Bull.	53
The Goat-foot God.	71

Part Three
The Mysteries Of Sea And Moon

The Sea Priestess.	103
Moon Magic.	118

Introduction

As well as being one of the foremost occultists of her generation Dion Fortune loved writing, and apart from her many textbooks and articles, she put a great deal of herself and her teaching into fiction. This survey into the magical world of her short stories and novels brings out a number of aspects of occult teaching that, because of constraints of occult secrecy pertaining at the time, were less explicitly treated in her non-fiction. In her early fiction she sought to bring to public attention some of the lesser known aspects of the human mind; and in her later novels she tried to indicate practical applications to the theoretical side of occultism, and to provide an initiatory experience to imaginative readers.

Her fiction divides naturally into three phases. The first, represented by the *Dr Taverner* stories of 1922/3, and her first novel, *The Demon Lover* of 1927, deal largely with occultism as seen from the outside looking in. As is common at this stage of approach to the Portal of the Mysteries, there is no shortage of reported marvels and a ready acceptance of popular tradition. The intended readership has a bearing upon this, for these works were written to startle and entertain, with the general public in mind.

Her later novels, from 1935 on, have an altogether different intention and readership, and she herself has moved along in the meantime, having founded an initiatory school and written

The Mystical Qabalah. Although she hoped they would interest and instruct the public at large, their principal aim was to illustrate some principles of life as revealed by the Qabalah. These four novels may be grouped into two pairs, *The Winged Bull* and *The Goat-foot God* evoking the Mysteries of the Sun and Earth, and *The Sea Priestess* and *Moon Magic* evoking the Mysteries of the Sea and Moon.

Apart from the magical teaching that can be gleaned from their pages, they contain some of Dion Fortune's writing at its evocative best, where she brings to the reader, as only a practising occultist could, something of the feel of the inner tides and currents of the unseen worlds.

Gareth Knight

Part One

At The Portal Of The Mysteries

Chapter One
The Secrets Of Dr. Taverner

Dion Fortune's first published fiction consists of a series of short stories that appeared in the *Royal Magazine* in 1922 and which were later published in book form as *The Secrets of Dr Taverner*. Apart from providing popular entertainment they had an underlying purpose, which was to draw public attention to what she felt to be a neglected area of the human mind.

Dion Fortune took the possibility of an esoteric clinic very seriously, and when she married Dr. Thomas Penry Evans in 1927, one of their aims was to set up just such a kind of establishment with their combined expertise. For various practical reasons this did not come to pass, but the seriousness of their endeavour can be gauged from the papers they produced along this line, which have subsequently been published as *Principles of Esoteric Healing*.[1]

However, something of the unrealised ideal is to be found in *The Secrets of Dr Taverner* together with some concrete illustrations of her esoteric beliefs rendered into fictional form.

It will be helpful if we study the stories not in order of their appearance in the book but grouped by theme, of which there are three.

a) pathological aspects and criminal abuses of occultism;
b) illustrations of the theory of reincarnation at work;
c) illustrations of the impact of the world of faery.

---

[1] *Principles of Esoteric Healing*, Thoth Publications 2006

There is a certain degree of overlap in the stories, for none of these categories are water tight compartments but their grouping in this way will enable us to examine certain points they have in common, without unnecessary repetition.

Pathological aspects and criminal abuses

In this category we have five stories: Blood Lust; The Scented Poppies; The Death Hound; The Subletting of the Mansion; and The Power House.

Blood Lust is written up from an important experience in Dion Fortune's own life, the occasion she first met Dr. Theodore Moriarty.

She had been working in London as a psychotherapist for the Medico-Psychological Clinic and was called in to assist upon a case that baffled her until she saw Moriarty at work. The strange events she witnessed caused her to abandon conventional psychotherapy, as being inadequate to deal with some of the lesser known powers of the human mind.

A junior colleague at the Clinic was having trouble with a rather difficult and unusual case. It involved a young man who would seem to have been indulging in some alarming activity concerning a lust for blood, and which also had some paranormal aspects in that in his vicinity, soon after dogs in the neighbourhood had set up a mutual barking, doors would be flung open for no apparent cause.

Moriarty, who had a reputation as an occultist, had just returned from South Africa, where he had lived for a number of years, and in view of the paranormal features surrounding the case was invited to give his opinion.

When they had assembled at the young man's flat one evening, after witnessing the doors fly open and hearing the barking of the local dogs, Moriarty announced that an unseen presence had entered the room. The lights were lowered, and a dull glow could be seen in one corner which induced a tingling sensation if a hand were put within it. Moriarty, by force of will, eventually pinned this manifestation down and despatched it by a process of absorption into his own aura, the repercussion from which knocked him unconscious.

His efforts, however bizarre they may have seemed, appeared to be successful. The young man's psychological condition improved and he declared that he felt released from some kind of overshadowing presence, of which he had not talked for fear of being thought insane.

It appeared that a cousin of his, a young officer who had recently been returned, ostensibly shell shocked, from the Western Front, had narrowly escaped court martial for necrophilia. It also transpired that the two young men were in the midst of a homosexual relationship in the course of which the bed-ridden young officer had bitten his young cousin in the neck sufficiently severely to draw blood.

It was Moriarty's diagnosis that the root of the trouble was the earth-bound soul of a German soldier of Eastern European origin, with a practical knowledge of the vampire traditions of Transylvania, who had been maintaining a parasitic ghostly existence by feeding off the two young men as a source of etheric vitality.

The details of this case were such as to cause Dion Fortune to claim that her story based upon it had been written down rather than written up, in order to be fit for printing in a popular magazine.

In her published story there is no homosexual element (a criminal offence in itself in those days), and the protagonists of the tale are rendered as a young heterosexual couple not out of place in conventional romantic fiction. The man, recently returned from the war, finds that he has developed a morbid taste for fresh blood. This he sates by killing chickens and sheep but has increasing fears that this may extend to attacking human beings - with his girl friend likely to be the first in line. He nobly tries to give up their relationship but Taverner is called in by his fiancée, who is puzzled by his strange behaviour. Dr. Taverner, like the real life Moriarty, diagnoses the presence of the ghostly vampire and duly despatches it.

The Scented Poppies certainly takes us from the world of psychic pathologies to the deliberate abuse of occult principles by a criminally minded occultist.

A succession of beneficiaries to a large estate have commited suicide, one after the other in much the same way, by jumping from a height. The instigator of this strange sequence of events, by a process of elimination, appears to be the individual who will eventually benefit from the coveted inheritance. The method that he uses is telepathic suggestion.

This kind of thing is of course easier said than done. In Taverner's view, thought transference requires more effort than swinging a sledge hammer, so if anyone is ever offered the choice between being an occultist or a blacksmith, he advises entering the forge as being the lighter job.

Nonetheless the villain in this case has found a mental labour saving device that works by giving a large bouquet of ornamental oriental poppy heads to his victims, for home decoration. These have a peculiar heavy scent, and it turns out that within each one of them is concealed some grains of a drug that tends to enhance psychic perception. Together with this there is a crystal that has been impressed with a telepathic image relating to suicide by flinging oneself from a height.

However, having discovered the means whereby these virtual murders are being committed Taverner is faced with the problem of what to do about it. For as he remarks, he is hardly likely to be taken seriously if he goes to a police station with such a tale, let alone convince a jury if it came to trial.

He declines to take the law into his own hands by a form of counter suggestion, for the evidence remains only circumstantial. He therefore hits upon a solution that will not harm the suspect if he should turn out to be innocent but will give him a very bad time if he should be guilty.

Knowing the man to be interested in occultism, he offers to open up his clairvoyant faculties for him. The offer is eagerly accepted but the consequences are drastic, for the wretched individual runs screaming into the night, first running towards the river to throw himself in, and then away from it into the busy streets as he realises that the horror that confronts him will still be waiting for him after his death. The horrific vision is the state of his own soul, known as the Dweller or Guardian on the Threshold in esoteric terminology.

In the case of an ordinary individual, neither very good nor very bad, Taverner remarks, this vision may turn out to be a somewhat disturbing but nonetheless enriching experience. In the case of a man capable of serial murder by occult means however, the experience is likely to be terrifying indeed.

The Death Hound also concerns the abuse of telepathic suggestion. In this case it is a matter of direct use of thought power by a highly trained occultist, with the motive being sexual rather than pecuniary.

The villain of the piece is playing a double game. On the one hand hypnotically fascinating the lady of his desires, and on the other sending a big black astral hound to frighten his rival, who has a weak heart.

The victim realises that the hound is not real, but nonetheless finds its presence terrifying. On one occasion, walking across the moors alone, he feels that it is stalking him, and almost succumbs to heart failure in his panic stricken flight.

The girl's experience is rather different. Despite feeling repelled and horrified by the physical presence of the occultist, in his absence she feels as if she is desperately in love with him. What is more, she finds herself agreeing, on an overwhelming impulse, to become engaged to marry him.

In this case Taverner intervenes by thought power on his own account. By superior thought control, he turns the astral hound back upon the one who sent it, who is last seen running across the moors in terror from the imaginary beast. Next day his exhausted body is found, with no marks of violence, but his heart has given out from the strain. "Six miles!" says Taverner. "He ran well!"

In ***The Subletting of the Mansion*** an occultist who happens to have the rare power to project himself in the etheric body is terminally ill with tuberculosis but also happens to lust after his neighbour's wife. The neighbour is comfortably wealthy and in good health but happens also to be a drug addict. The occultist therefore decides that when the addict is projected out of his body by narcotics, he will to use his little known occult powers to leave his own body and enter that of his neighbour's before he has chance to return to it. Thus his neighbour will be left stranded on the astral plane whilst he himself will achieve a healthy body and the sexual partner of his choice in one fell swoop.

Once again we have the situation of an occultist of low moral integrity able to flout the law because his knowledge and abilities are not recognised by the legal or scientific establishment. However, Taverner foretells that little good will result from these deeds. That the soul forced out of incarnation will hang about as an earth bound spirit, because its time for death has not come, obsessed with seeking revenge by some means or another.

On the other hand, the occultist himself may not long enjoy the advantage of good health, for according to Taverner's belief, tuberculosis is a disease generated in the soul and will thus soon break out again in the new body. More importantly, we might ask, what is the lady in the triangle going to make of all this and how much she is likely to know or to suspect? One might also expect that the drug soaked body that the occultist has taken over would remain with its addiction, although Taverner seems to think that the addiction is one of the soul rather than the body.

There are plenty of points to ponder therefore, both technical and moral. Taverner's conclusion is that there need be no special hell provided for those who dabble in forbidden things; it would be superfluous, for they make it for themselves.

The final story in the original volume of stories, **The Power House**, illustrates the difference between real and pseudo occultism. An establishment is run by a seedy character who has little real occult ability but a good grasp of the weakness in the psychology of those who may be attracted to the subject.

Like others of his type he fleeces his victims either financially or sexually, sometimes in quite subtle ways. As Taverner remarks, "an infatuated woman at any time is difficult to deal with, but when they have been initiated into a fraternity with ritual they are almost impossible." Nor need he have confined his remarks to the female sex.

The way in which Taverner and his assistant Rhodes deal with the situation is crude and illegal but nonetheless effective. They physically overpower the leader of the group, tie him up and dump him in the coal cellar, and then hi-jack his meeting.

Taverner, dressed in impressive ceremonial robes, ritually cleanses the altar with salt, and lectures the members sternly as to their aspirations and motives. As he says to the woman who has abandoned her husband to follow the man whom she thinks to be her spiritual leader: "You cannot advance - save by the path of duty. You cannot rise to the higher life on broken faith and neglected obligations."

In the real world the fake occultism of this last story is likely to be a far more common problem than the criminal activities illustrated in the others, which require rare abilities and conditions whose abuse is likely to be more theoretical than practical. Dion Fortune had a keen eye for the various common abuses of the esoteric world, that she wrote in a series of articles for *The Occult Review* that caused a considerable fluttering in the esoteric dove cots at the time. They were later published as *Sane Occultism*, recently reissued with the more anodyne title of *What Is Occultism?*[2]

---

[2] What Is Occultism? (Red Wheel/Weiser, 2003).

Reincarnation

In this category we have four stories: *The Return of the Ritual; The Man Who Sought; The Soul Who Would Not Be Born*; and *Recalled*.

Dion Fortune's experience of some of Moriarty's abilities feature in **The Return of the Ritual**, which sees Taverner throwing himself into deep trance in order to gain certain information. The story rests on the assumption that there are certain rituals so ancient and powerful that even to read them will cause certain vibrations to occur in the subtle ethers.

In one of his entranced sessions Taverner detects someone tinkering with an ancient ritual long believed to be lost. He takes steps to discover who the perpetrator might be, to provide restoration of the ritual to its rightful owners, in a series of events that unravel in a somewhat romantic and swashbuckling fashion.

The script in question originates in the Italian Renaissance, when at the time of Cosimo Medici and other powerful princes, great interest was generated in the Hermetic tradition. The sack of Byzantium by the Turks in 1453 had released many ancient manuscripts into the libraries of the courts of Europe. In Dion Fortune's story the ritual has now turned up in the second hand book trade, purchased by a collector, whose reading of it attracted the attention of Taverner.

When Taverner "goes subconscious" as he calls it, he aims to penetrate to "the level of the Records", examining the subconscious mind of the human race where, he says, every thought and every act have their images stored in the mind of Nature. This is something of an extension upon Jung's idea of the collective unconscious.

By these means Taverner is able to trace the identity of the 15th century Florentine who first stole the ritual manuscript and also to establish that he is now reincarnated as a London bank clerk. Having established this, he is able to lodge suggestions into the subconscious mind of the modern young man, who, because of the particularly strong emotive and historical links he has with the stolen manuscript, will be able to intuit its present location and take steps to gain possession of it, probably driven to impulsive and irrational means.

Sure enough a news item soon appears, reporting that a certain Peter Robson, through what he describes as an irresistible urge, has broken into the house of a collector and stolen a recently purchased manuscript, but because of his lack of expertise in burglary was apprehended in the act. Taverner attends the magistrate's court, and by claiming to be the young man's medical practitioner and going surety for him succeeds in getting his release.

In the meantime, in this very picaresque tale, some black magicians have got wind of what is going on and have stolen the manuscript for themselves. Taverner resolves the situation by the novel and illegal means of inducing Robson to locate the ritual once more and steal it back.

In view of his proven lack of criminal expertise hypnotically regresses Robson back to his previous Florentine personality of Pierro della Costa which brings about a startling transformation. Power seems to radiate from him, even his features seemed changed, and the eyes of the humble bank clerk take on the glitter of steel of a Renaissance adventurer and swordsman. In a daring raid he recovers the manuscript back from the black magicians and is driven at high speed down to Southampton to make his final getaway.

At Southampton docks, a sea captain recognises certain signs in his aura, and offers him a clandestine passage to West Africa. On the African quayside he makes a certain sign, whereupon a local native approaches and leads him away into the crowd. There is no need to worry over his safety, the sea captain remarks, for that secret sign would take him right across Africa and back again.

There is behind this unlikely story the assumption that an initiate of an esoteric order will be infallibly protected and guided. Although there may be truth in this at a certain level, for significant coincidence and the recognition of strangers can play an important part at key moments in occultists' lives, membership of an esoteric group should not be assumed to bring quite such universal benefits as this popular presentation might lead one to suppose.

The Man Who Sought concerns the case of a man with an overwhelming obsession. A keen sporting motorist and aviator, he has the vision of some kind of lost love whom he cannot identify. It simply induces him to drive at breakneck speed, usually to the coast, in order to find her.

The obsession first came upon him after an air accident when, after a spinning nose dive, he was knocked unconscious and lay in a coma for three days. During the spin he had felt as if a pair of eyes were upon him, and when he eventually came round he had the overwhelming feeling of being in love – but with whom he did not know. He also begins to have confused dreams which seem to take place in bright sunshine and to have a vaguely oriental flavour.

By showing him a number of historical pictures Taverner establishes that these dreams seem to be somehow related to ancient Egypt, and concludes that the spinning of the aircraft in the accident induced an hypnotic state that regressed his patient to some crucial point in time. That is, to another incarnation, probably Egyptian, and strongly associated with the female whom he now obsessively seeks.

By further research Taverner discovers that this person is currently alive, fortunately in the body of a young unmarried woman of compatible social and educational background. It transpires that she too is subject to irrational obsessions. She sometimes has the strong feeling that there is a man in her room, or that someone is calling her, which leads her to take long walks, often at night, seeking for she knows not whom.

As the consequence of a dramatic coincidence the two finally meet in Taverner's nursing home. She has been taken in for observation, while he has crashed his car nearby and is brought in for surgical treatment. As he lies at death's door, she, in her room nearby, becomes highly excited, saying that she can feel her familiar mysterious presence close by.

With the lights lowered, it is possible to observe a grey mist building up over her bed. As it slowly takes form it can be recognised to have the features of the injured man in the bed down the corridor - Arnold Black. Taverner realises that this is an etheric projection from the injured motorist, who will die unless it retains its link to his physical body. He persuades the girl to walk slowly down the corridor to the injured man's room, and to his relief the grey mist follows her.

She does not consciously recognise the man she finds lying before her, but gently takes his bruised and broken body into her arms, and as she does so the etheric mist is gradually reabsorbed into his physical form.

This is but the preliminary to a romantic relationship and the marriage of the couple six weeks later. Taverner's assistant remarks that most doctors would say that he had mated a couple of lunatics whose delusions happened to match, to which Taverner replies that at least that is preferable to confining the pair of them to an asylum as most of his colleagues would have done.

He claims that all he has done is to recognise the working of two great laws. Having looked at the history of their past lives, he found that they had a spiritual tie, and had been mated in life after life. In the Egyptian incarnation however, she had been a princess of the royal house while he was a mere soldier of fortune. As a consequence, when their illicit relationship was discovered he was thrown from the roof of the palace to his death. This death experience had been restimulated by the spinning nose dive in the plane crash, which sparked his current obsession.

On the other hand, whilst Miss Tyndall's delusions might have seemed like a commonplace case of "old maid's insanity", her self-possession, absence of fear, and impersonal attitude toward her delusions suggested that something more was involved.

This provided an explanation of their problem in esoteric terms, although the chance of their coming together involved highly unlikely coincidence. But as far as that is concerned, Taverner simply looks up at the stars and suggests that the ultimate truth may rest there.

A less fortunate outcome to a reincarnationary tale is to be found in **The Soul That Would Not Be Born**. It is a case of what would nowadays be regarded as a severe form of autism, in a young woman who seems to have undergone no mental development whatever since birth.

Her mother reports that when she was born the child had the most extraordinary expression in her eyes, that of a mature and experienced woman. She did not cry but gave the impression of having all the troubles of the world weighing in upon her. After a few hours this expression disappeared and she appeared to be just like any other baby, but despite developing physically into a normal healthy adult, she had never developed mentally.

Taverner takes her under observation in the hope of finding some clue to her condition by investigating her previous incarnations. If brain damage is the cause he admits he will be able to do nothing, but there might be some hope if the trouble lies simply in the mind. The crux of the problem rests in trying to establish communication with her.

Taverner makes no apology for using astrology, crystal gazing or hypnosis when occasion seems to demand it, but in this case he decides to go into trance to consult the akashic records. In his search he comes upon her in life after life either of royal birth or of the initiated priesthood until, in 15th century Italy, she turns out to be a real daughter of the Renaissance, seducing her sister's lover and then betraying him, with the result that he is tortured to death.

In the immediate pre-birth condition, he explains, a soul sees in broad outline a kind of cinematograph film of its future life. In his view the soul of the young woman foresaw a life in which the karmic debts of the immediate past would have to be repaid. Horrified by the prospect, she rebelled and virtually refused to incarnate.

According to Taverner, it was now simply a question of watching and waiting for events to take their course, presumably by some significant coincidence. This duly comes about through a shell shocked soldier from the war, who is also a patient at the nursing home. He is subject to the most terrible nightmares and visions, but finds comfort in the presence of the autistic girl, who in turn begins to show some kind of awakening to life in his presence.

In the course of time this brings sufficient recovery in the young man for his fiancée to arrive to take him away from the nursing home. This precipitates a painful crisis for the autistic girl, who has become sufficiently aware to realise that she is about to lose the one personal contact she has ever been able to make. Nonetheless, somehow she apparently realises not only its inevitability but its justification.

For such a simple story line a considerable amount of moral evaluation needs to be taken into account in this tale. It is an illustration of the law of karma in its simplest, most basic form, that the mis-doings of one life will lead to affliction of one kind or another in a later one. In the modern western world despite a greater openness to oriental ideas, it is a doctrine that many would find repugnant. Are those afflicted by misfortune only getting what they deserve from misdeeds in a previous life?

There are, however, special circumstances in this particular case, it would seem. Mona Cailey, the autistic young woman, is a soul of a high and special kind, and Taverner is led to say, in a tone of hyperbole unusual for him, that she is more than royal, that she is an Initiate - in tones which suggests that by this he refers to a form of royalty that is not of this earth. In a highly unusual sequence we find Taverner overseeing her renewing contact with her spiritual peers on the inner side.

One is left to wonder however, how it was that such a high initiate could have been so morally delinquent in a recent incarnation. Or perhaps the adventures of the soul are more complex than we think.

The story in **Recalled** is concerned with a very recent case of reincarnation, and again in association with a very advanced soul. Sexual morality also comes into it, compounded by racial prejudice and social convention in the context of a British imperial theme.

A member of the British raj in India has had a sexual liaison with a fifteen year old native girl. However, when she became pregnant with his child he abandoned her. As a consequence she committed suicide, thus bringing about the death of the unborn child too.

The pillar of Anglo-Indian society has now married an English lady of his own class but the two of them call upon Taverner in some distress. The wife has recently become interested in occultism but finds herself being obsessed with the presence of a young native woman who seems to be seeking some kind of retribution. This has preyed on her mind so much that she has lost all vitality and is laid low with what seems like some form of sleepy sickness. The husband of course has told his wife nothing of his previous affair, but all comes out under Taverner's questioning.

It turns out that the soul to which the native girl was destined to give birth is a highly evolved spiritual being who requires incarnation via a union of mixed blood the better to fulfil a destiny of helping to bridge the cultural divide between east and west.

On these facts being painfully brought to light both husband and wife agree that they owe a moral debt to the unborn child and to its destiny in the world. Once they realise this, the wife quickly recovers from her malaise and within a year a child is born to them. They have in the meantime returned to India but on furlough some five years later they call upon Dr Taverner, bringing with them their child.

It is a little boy with jet black hair, dark olive skin, slender limbs, and a pair of eyes as blue as the sea, the eyes of the West in a face of the East. Moreover they are described as the strangest eyes to be seen in the face of a child, as if containing the depth of the sea as well as its blueness. Taverner's reaction is unequivocal. As the child forms an instant rapport with him he proclaims it as "One of Us!", that is to say of the spiritual status of an initiate.

The world of faery

In this category we have three stories: *A Daughter of Pan; The Sea Lure* and *Son of the Night*.

A Daughter of Pan is a charming little story about a couple who, in the nineteen sixties, would have been regarded as fairly commonplace hippies. However, in the era of these stories, the nineteen twenties, when Taverner is quite commonly found to be wearing a top hat, social structures and attitudes were considerably more rigid.

The couple concerned are a girl called Diana, a total misfit as far as her wealthy country family is concerned, and Tennant, a desperately introverted musician from a highly unartistic family. There is something about these two, moreover, that is not entirely human. Diana's flashing green eyes and elfin smile, and Tennant's somewhat pointed ears give some hint of this.

In the nursing home, left to her own devices Diana dresses up in an old stage costume of Puck from *A Midsummer Night's Dream* and wants to be taken for runs like a dog. While Tennant, pressed to play the piano, performs classical pieces like an emotionless automaton, but when given an old violin, tunes it to his own strange harmonies, and improvises haunting melodies that seem to change the atmosphere.

If there are such beings as changelings, or humans part faery or closely related to them in some way, then Diana and Tennant are examples of such. Taverner, being inclined to this theory, pushes Diana out into the wilds of the countryside at the Vernal Equinox with a view to seeing if she will link up with her own non-human kin. This she appears to do, somewhat to the disturbance of Rhodes, Dr. Taverner's assistant, who is partly seduced by the call of the wild that this child of nature induces in him. He realises however that a close relationship with Diana is not a way that is wise for him, for although he finds a strange attraction in her call, there is much within her that, as a normal human being, he knows he would be incapable of meeting.

Fortunately this is not the case with Tennant, who from being suicidal and repressed opens out in response to Diana's own self realisation. The Summer Solstice sees them taking to the woods and finding fulfilment in each other. Their first coming together is evocatively told by Rhodes. How Tennant, propped against a tree, hat off, shirt open, and head thrown back against the rough red bark, sits gazing into the blue distance and whistling softly between his teeth while Diana softly approaches and lies at his feet, gazing into his face with the unblinking steadiness of an animal, as he continues whistling softly with an exquisite, flute-like tone, strange cadences that seem to evoke an older world of the centaurs and titans. The two are obviously of the same world and belong to each other.

The story concludes with their marriage, striding off into the sunset accompanied by a donkey upon whose back is packed a tent and a range of cooking pots. The following Spring Rhodes is called out into the woods to attend the birth of a child, although his assistance is little needed, as he delivers the baby, perfectly normal save for its tufted ears!

This story is an important fore-runner to some of Dion Fortune's later fiction, particularly *The Goat-Foot God*. Something of the deeper powers of her vision and lyrical description of it are to be found here, as for example when Diana first goes out into the countryside at the Vernal Equinox to meet her own people. A scene that Dion Fortune compares in atmosphere to that of Kipling's *Jungle Book* when the wolf cubs are taken to the Council Rock.

Rhodes describes how the wind dropped and as the full moon sailed across the heavens in a golden haze of cloud a nearby stream sounded very loud in the stillness. He heard and saw nothing but knew that something was coming towards them through the shadow of the wood. He found himself trembling in every limb, not from fear, but excitement. Something was passing, something big and massive, and in its train many lesser things of the same nature. Every nerve in his body began to sing, and without any volition, one foot took a step forward. But Taverner's hand on his arm restrained him, saying "This is not for you Rhodes. You have too much mentality to find your mating here."

A little later he again finds himself caught up in the faery rout as he vainly pursues Diana until he drops to the ground gasping. As he lies helpless in the heather he senses a great streaming procession like an undisciplined army, passing across the sky. Ragged banners flap and wave, wild, discordant, maddening music breaks here and there from the motley rout. Furry snouts on human faces, clawed paws on human limbs, green, vine-like hair falling over flashing eyes that gleam as green, and here and there, half-frightened, half-fascinated human faces, some hanging back though lured along, others giving themselves up to the flight in a wild abandonment. He awakes to find Taverner bending over him with the words, "Thank God, your eyes are still human."

The Sea Lure also has its elemental side, although its main purpose exemplifies occult traditions about the projection of the etheric body, including the possibility of repercussion upon the physical body should any mishap befall it. Taverner is called in to advise upon a case of a girl suffering from shot gun wounds but without any physical shots having been fired. It all seems as mysterious as the appearance of stigmata upon the saints.

The girl in question, although living the life of a London shop assistant, has a strong elemental side to her nature and is particularly attracted to the sea. She is also of great physical beauty after the style of a Pre-Raphaelite painting.

The source of the trouble turns out to be an occultist who has come to the conclusion that he has too much Earth element in his nature and not enough Water and has commenced upon an occult experiment to remedy this defect. He is currently living as a recluse in a lonely cottage overlooking the sea, the better to meditate upon the Powers of Water. The imbalance in his nature may well be indicated in his astrological birth chart but would also appear to be painfully demonstrated in his very literal turn of mind in magical terms, and his inability to deal with the emotional side of his life.

This combination comes to the fore when, in the course of his meditations, he thinks he sees an elemental creature swimming in the sea before him. She seems somehow to be calling to him, with an attraction he finds increasingly difficult to resist. Accordingly, as a consequence of the almost pathological earthiness of his nature, he obtains a gun, loads it with silver bullets, to take shots at the visitant when it next appears.

The being however is no mermaid seeking to lure him to his death but the etheric body of the London shop girl, unconsciously projecting herself during sleep into the waves, drawn there by the invocations of the hapless occultist, which are more effective than he realises. The silver bullets are effective too, for they cause repercussions on the girl's physical body to the astonishment of the doctors in the London hospital.

The solution proves much the same as in *The Daughter of Pan* and *The Man Who Sought*. The two misfits are introduced to each other, soon fall into each other's arms, and appear set to live happily ever after.

The final story, **A Son of the Night**, did not appear in the original book of collected stories, so its date of origin is uncertain. Its first publication was in the *Inner Light Magazine* in 1938, and it is possible that it is an early story that was left incomplete and finished at a later date. It does seem something of a hybrid work, although nonetheless interesting for that.

Its theme is principally of initiation, that of Taverner's assistant Dr Rhodes, but it has a strong elemental slant in the character who is largely responsible for opening his eyes to the existence and reality of the inner planes.

This character is the inheritor of a stately home who is something of an eccentric, upsetting members of his family by refusing to indulge their social whims and ambitions. They decide to try to have him certified as insane, but unfortunately for them the local doctor will not accede to their plan. Even more unfortunately for them, in search of a second opinion they turn to Dr. Taverner.

Taverner immediately recognises Lord Cullan as a kindred spirit, and he is certainly a complex and fascinating man. Whilst he has a certain kinship with the Elemental beings of the other stories, *Daughter of Pan* and *The Sea Lure*, he is somehow a great deal broader than any of them. It is almost as if he is an incarnation of the spirit of the land that he owns.

A sub-plot suggests that he may be the son, not of his aristocratic mother, but of a half-gypsy girl who was beloved by his father. Be this as it may, the local vicar refuses to grant him the sacraments, whilst he himself wanders about the countryside, consorting with gypsies, and develops a reputation for bewitching crops. Nonetheless he is welcomed by the country people wherever he goes, who welcome him in for a meal or a drink. In return he seems to act as a kind of mascot at harvest and ploughing time, who invite him in to cut the first swathe at haying or to walk in the furrow at seeding.

Here Taverner's assistant Rhodes begins to develop a personal awareness of the unseen world. Until now he has only been a more or less sympathetic onlooker upon Taverner's activities but in this story he begins to look at things more from the inside, and indeed to cross the threshold of initiatory experience.

When Lord Cullan meets Rhodes for the first time he gives him a kind of mock baptism, conferring another name on him, whilst reaching up to the branch of a birch tree above them, to shake down a shower of rain drops from a storm that has just passed. Taverner has invited Lord Cullan to stay at his nursing home, ostensibly for observation, which brings him more in contact with Rhodes, although it begins to be a little unclear who is supposed to be treating whom.

In the company of Cullan Rhodes finds himself undergoing a subtle change of consciousness, as well as to realise that Cullan and Taverner, although different in many ways, have certain qualities in common. The best that he can put it is that "they both came from the same spiritual place in the hinterland of the subconscious." And a process of dawning realisation begins to take place in himself.

This comes to a crisis when he is attending a formal dinner of medical colleagues. He suddenly realises the huge gap in awareness that exists between himself and them. Leaving the event in a state of some turmoil he drives down through the night onto the Sussex downs. Here he pulls up to meditate within the shadow of a great Keltic cross upon a hill – ever a symbol of initiation for Dion Fortune.

Here he comes to realise that he has passed through an invisible barrier. Whilst the outside world is unchanged, there has become a profound difference in his awareness of it. All things have suddenly become alive. And not only are they alive, but they share in their life with him, for he is at one with them. He finally sums it up: "and then I knew that, isolated though I must always be in the world of men, I had this infinite companionship all about me. I was no longer alone, for, like Taverner, Marius, and many others, I had passed over into the Unseen."

Chapter Two

The Demon Lover

The Story

An occult society that has devoted itself to a scholarly study of comparative religious and mythological lore has, in recent years, developed an interest in the practical side of occultism, becoming a high powered occult fraternity with grades of initiation and secret rituals.

Its secretary, Justin Lucas, has been largely responsible for this change, although some senior members of the society are concerned about how far he can be trusted, and suspect him of vaulting spiritual ambition. He has therefore been prevented from entering the higher grades, which provokes him to try to discover their secrets by clandestine means.

He would like to spy upon the performance of their higher rituals from the astral plane but doubts if he has the ability to do it himself, and in any case does not relish the consequences of being detected in the act. He therefore decides to find an intermediary, a psychic under his hypnotic control, who if discovered would be the one to suffer any unpleasant repercussions.

He seeks a vulnerable girl with natural psychic ability who is likely to be a docile hypnotic subject, and with this in mind advertises for a residential secretarial assistant at the fraternity's headquarters. He finds a likely candidate in Veronica Mainwaring, a genteel creature, alone in the world, with little experience of life beyond caring for an invalid mother. Taken on by Lucas, she soon falls victim to his hypnotic powers, and having thrown her into trance, he sends her out on astral journeys as his psychic spy.

It is not long before her presence is detected and the punitive ray of the fraternity is about to be evoked upon the unknown watcher. Lucas however, until now a selfish loner, has begun to feel tenderly for Veronica, and tries to prevent her becoming a victim of the fraternity's vengeance. In a dramatic confrontation, he reveals himself to be the real guilty party, and in an endeavour to escape from the consequences flees to a remote hideaway in the country, taking Veronica with him.

Here he hopes to lie low until perhaps the brothers relent or give up on failing to find him but the astral hunting hounds are soon heard baying in the vicinity. Lucas retires to his room and in the morning is found apparently dead. His body is duly buried in the local churchyard.

This is not the end of Lucas however. It appears that he has enough occult knowledge and power to maintain a ghostly earthbound existence, although he needs to find the energy from somewhere to hold his subtle body together - an energy that can only be obtained from the living. He gets a certain amount from Veronica herself, in the form of ectoplasm as in a séance, but this is not enough without depleting her dangerously. He is therefore driven to try to draw vital energy from young children as they sleep but badly overdoes this etheric vampirism and brings about a spate of infant mortality in the village.

As if this were not bad enough, Lucas also shows himself capable of direct and overt malice. He is overcome with jealousy when a young man of the village takes a romantic interest in Veronica. He therefore overshadows a large mastiff dog, which attacks the young man and savages him to death. Events have now become seriously out of hand.

In an attempt to resolve the mounting problem they have in part engendered, some senior members of the fraternity now appear on the scene. They seek a solution by the somewhat bizarre means of evoking a storm that causes a flood that washes the coffin out of the ground; thus they succeed in retrieving Lucas's body. Their purpose is to deal with the vampire in traditional fashion by the grisly method of driving a stake through its heart but to their surprise find that Lucas is not dead. On hearing the approach of the astral hounds he had thrown himself into a cataleptic trance, after the fashion of certain yogis, in the hope that eventually he might be exhumed and revivified.

This was obviously a high risk strategy, the more so as Lucas has failed to take account of the fact that before burial his body might be subjected to post mortem examination. Such has been the case, and although he seems not greatly inconvenienced by the loss of certain viscera, his eyes have been removed, rendering him permanently blind.

However, a strong karmic link existing between him and Veronica now comes into play. It seems that they have been linked together in life after life, although their association in this life has been a strange and unfortunate one. This is due to certain events that occurred in Imperial Rome and later in the middle ages at Avignon, when the soul of Lucas had diverted onto the Left-hand Path. Veronica now feels impelled to return the love that had begun to stir in Lucas and undertakes to care for him for the rest of their days. Lucas is now a wiser and repentant man, and they start their new life together in the belief that in future lives they will be re-united in happier fashion in mutual pursuit of their spiritual evolution.

* * *

Dion Fortune's first full length novel, *The Demon Lover,* like most of the Dr. Taverner stories, is obviously of the popular "blood and thunder" kind, her main purpose being to make the general public aware of the unseen worlds by means of an occult thriller with a romantic love interest.

In an article written in 1936, when she had embarked upon her more serious novels, she wrote that the purpose of the Taverner stories had been very near the surface, simply to point out the possibilities that occult knowledge might have in applications of psychotherapy. Her first novel, on the other hand, set out to be a thriller pure and simple but in the course of writing had developed a theme of the purification of a soul through initiation.

Actually Lucas, who undergoes this redemption, seems already to be an initiate of some advancement, even if he seeks to apply his occult knowledge in less than scrupulous ways. His purification comes about, not through secret rituals of high initiation that he aspires to, but through the power of human love.

The spiritual progress he makes, (at the cost of no small suffering to others as well as himself) might well be considered a higher form of initiation, but it is an initiation of love and life, rather than of the occult lodge as narrowly understood.

Like the stories in *The Secrets of Dr. Taverner*, the plot of *The Demon Lover* is the vehicle for a body of various esoteric theories and practice, reflecting much of Dion Fortune's personal beliefs and experience during the first dozen years of her occult career.

The sequence of events in this somewhat grisly tale provides a vehicle for a number of esoteric beliefs and topics that we might list and consider as:

Esoteric fraternities;
Trance mediumship;
Reincarnation and Karma;
Occult techniques and technicalities (hypnosis, etheric projection, etc).

Esoteric Fraternities

The esoteric fraternity within the novel exists only in the pages of fiction, but as a society largely devoted to obscure branches of ancient and speculative learning it has a similarity with a number of Victorian organisations, of which perhaps the most prominent was the Societas Rosicruciana in Anglia, which still exists as a respectable and learned institution today. It was largely from its members that the more practically oriented Hermetic Order of the Golden Dawn drew its founders in 1888.

The fraternity to which Lucas belongs is thus, in a certain sense, a paradigm of what has been a general historical movement in western esoteric circles. The Golden Dawn split into various smaller organisations and Dion Fortune was initiated into a surviving branch of it in 1919.

Although in *The Secrets of Dr Taverner* we have found that initiates (especially if spelt with a capital I) tend to be regarded with some awe and reverence, there have also been some aspirants or claimants to the condition who have fallen very far short of the mark. The same is found in *The Demon Lover*.

Lucas can hardly be regarded as a very laudable specimen. He has successfully wormed his way into the corridors of power with the intention of becoming, if not top dog, then very close to the small controlling oligarchy. And if he cannot gain advancement by fair means then he will do so by foul.

Another senior member of the fraternity is Dr. Latimer, a benevolent old man who means well but is an easy dupe for Lucas, and he comes to regret his patronage of this unscrupulous young man in a hurry.

Then there is Fordyce, the Magus of the mysterious Seventh Degree, the grade upon which Veronica is charged to spy. Whilst nominally on the side of virtue, he reveals himself to be self righteous, opinionated and irascible, and is dismissed from participation in the final stages of the work for these very reasons.

These could well have been drawn from the life, as composite characters based on various individuals on the esoteric scene in Dion Fortune's day. She was not prone to pull her punches when it came to denouncing follies and abuses and in a series of articles in *The Occult Review* during the 1920's did just that, to the chagrin and anger of some of her contemporaries. These articles were later collected in volume form as *Sane Occultism*, recently republished with the more anodyne title of *What is Occultism?* [1]

On the credit side however, another initiate appears who rises above these all too human foibles. He is evidently a very senior member of the fraternity, in fact so senior that he seldom makes an appearance at their meetings and only turns up here, it would seem, because of the great crisis in the fraternity's affairs. He is not addressed by name and is simply referred to as "The Third".

This would suggest, not simply a member of a higher degree within the Fraternity, but a member of a higher Order altogether. This interesting conception reflects a teaching of the Golden Dawn which thought in terms of three Orders of initiation. The First Order conferred initiations at lower level and gave public lectures and teaching. The Second Order consisted of adepti only, that is to say those considered to be proven practitioners of the occult arts, whether or not their supposed status was supported by the facts. The Third Order was that of the Secret Chiefs, in Golden Dawn terminology, who correspond to the Theosophists' idea of Masters, and to those whom 17th century Rosicrucians referred to as "governors of the world". Dion Fortune's school came to prefer the term Inner Plane Adepti.

Insofar that "The Third" also refers to himself as "the Count" we might take the hint that in this character we have some kind of epiphany of the Master Rakoczi who, as Dion Fortune well knew, is sometimes referred to by this title.

---

[1] *What is Occultism?* (Weiser/Red Wheel, 2003).

In terms of the Qabalistic Tree of Life, the diagrammatic yardstick of much western esoteric teaching, the First Order might be said to refer to the functional triad immediately above Malkuth, that is to say the spheres of Yesod, Netzach and Hod – and to be concerned with the control of the personality in everyday life. The Second Order thereby refers to the triad of Tiphareth, Geburah and Chesed, which is that of the Higher Self, the part of the self that lasts for a whole evolution and projects a succession of personalities into the outer world, whilst the Third Order relates to the spiritual spheres of Binah, Chokmah and Kether beyond the worlds of form.

It has ever been a bone of contention in esoteric circles whether such elevated beings maintain a presence upon the physical plane or not. Some favour a remote physical location such as the high Himalayas or the Andes, others prefer subtler levels of the physical ethers. But plainly for the purposes of Dion Fortune's story the Count is capable of arriving physically to take a direct hand in things – although the respect shown to him by Latimer and Fordyce indicate that this is no common occurrence.

Whatever the shortcomings that may be found in organisations representative of the First or Second Orders, they should not detract from the possibility of a wholly admirable Third Order that interrelates with the great army of prophets, mystics and illuminati throughout the ages.

Dion Fortune perhaps comes closest to an appreciation of what an esoteric fraternity should be all about in *The Esoteric Orders and their Work* and *The Training and Work of an Initiate* which she wrote soon after this early fiction, when she had founded her own Fraternity.

It hardly needs saying that secretaries of esoteric societies are not in the habit of carrying revolvers to meetings, let alone threatening their colleagues with one. But the episode in *The Demon Lover* where Lucas indulges in this kind of behaviour is simply an irresistible opportunity for Dion Fortune to end a chapter with the dramatic punch line – "You can put up your weapon, Mr. Lucas. We shall not use *physical* force." He then knows he is up against the dreaded "Dark Ray of Destruction"!

Trance Mediumship

Dion Fortune's descriptions of trance derive from observing Theodore Moriarty, her first occult teacher, who was apparently skilled in this technique. She provides more details of this in her semi-autobiographical *Psychic Self Defence* published in 1930.

We have seen in *The Secrets of Dr. Taverner* her descriptions of trance as a means of making contact with various levels of consciousness in the past or present in pursuit of therapeutic diagnosis. In *The Demon Lover* she presents a more prosaic version, where at a fairly routine business meeting, one of the members of the committee lies on a couch in full trance acting as a kind of trans-Atlantic telephone. Nowadays, with fax, the internet, and satellite transmission, science would seem to have more than caught up with these wonders of the psychic world of yesteryear. Even Madame Blavatsky's famed Mahatma Letters might, if sent nowadays, benefit from being transmitted by more reliable and less controversial means than "psychic precipitation".

The brothers are concerned about a renegade member who has been dabbling in international finance and we learn that he has been duly dealt with by means of the Dark Ray of Destruction. This has resulted in him committing suicide by jumping from a bridge near Niagara Falls. Whilst such concerns are hardly an accurate reflection of the activities of a real life esoteric society, this melodramatic interchange serves to alert us to the fact that, at any rate in occult fiction, there might be psychic ways and means of being very unpleasant to anyone who kicks over the traces of esoteric discipline. Upon this, and its consequences, the story largely depends.

Talk of Punitive Currents or Dark Rays of Destruction were part and parcel of the Golden Dawn tradition, perhaps as a consequence of the blood curdling oaths inherited from Freemasonic tradition. Certainly at the time when she was writing her early fiction Dion Fortune believed such things to be true, as did many of her contemporaries. She confirms this in *Psychic Self-Defence* and something of the background material is also provided in my biography *Dion Fortune and the Inner Light*[2]. The end result, it should be said, seemed one of general emotional unpleasantness rather than drastic psycho-physical results, although some mention of the strange behaviour of local cats plays its part. Hints of possible foul play in the strange death of her friend Netta Fornario on Iona hardly pass beyond circumstantial conjecture.

However, Dion Fortune was no mere observer of trance phenomena, and went to considerable pains to develop the ability herself. Some at least of Veronica's experiences in trance may thus be quite close accounts of the author's own. In addition a great deal more material along these lines from her non-fictional and private papers has now been collated and published as *Spiritualism and Occultism*.[3]

Not that Dion Fortune is likely to have had anything like the fictional experience of being forcibly hypnotised into trance like her heroine Veronica Mainwaring. It is interesting to note that when Lucas sends Veronica out in full trance for three or four nights each week, in sessions that last from dusk until dawn, she is said to suffer no fatigue from this, for physically she was in a state of deep sleep. Dion Fortune claims much the same from her own experience, and although she never appears to have worked continuously from dusk until dawn, her records show that trance communications of several hours duration were not uncommon.

---

[2] *Dion Fortune and the Inner Light* (Thoth Publications, 2000).
[3] *Spiritualism and Occultism* (Thoth Publications, 1999).

In her enforced psychic work Veronica begins to feel a benign Presence. The ambience seems to be of a formidable but well loved teacher, watching over her as she is sent out on her astral journeys. In this we may have a replication of Dion Fortune's experience of the beneficence and reliability of her own contacts, together with an overriding Christ contact behind, a belief in which Dion Fortune ever maintained, despite her latterly becoming an icon of the neo-pagan movement.

With increased experience Veronica becomes less completely psychically passive and begins to be able to recall some of her out of body experiences, dimly aware of being present while great rituals are being enacted. This is described as a tenuous silver thread which connects her soul with the body left behind under Lucas's care. Down this thread the impressions received by her soul are transmitted to the physical brain at the other end and acted out under its direction. The words she hears in projected trance stimulate a reflective activity in the vocal cords of the distant throat, and the actions of the prime mover in the ceremonial are repeated by the vacated body. All this while, her volitional consciousness in abeyance, she figuratively lies back, as if in deep blue water, and observes, as a disinterested spectator, that which her soul perceives and conveys to her brain. This is very much in line with details of Dion Fortune's own recorded experiences.

Aspects of the more frightening side of Veronica's experiences may well also reflect Dion Fortune's own, when in her early experiments thrills and spills seemed not unknown. When Veronica awakes to find herself on the floor with Lucas gripping her wrists striving to hold her down, the situation seems much like the phenomena recorded in *Psychic Self-Defence* when Dion Fortune's entranced body arched convulsively around the room before she shot back to normal consciousness in a scattered circle of frightened occult beginners.

Dion Fortune maintained her practice of mediumship for the whole of her life and indeed considered it essential for the working of an esoteric group, helping to imbue it with inner power. This was undoubtedly the case in her own day, although in the ensuing half century other techniques have been proven to be as valid, and less reliant upon one central star performer as a source of authority in a group. One of these methods is to be found in ceremonial work, some dynamics of which feature in her later novels, and about which she also wrote in various articles that have been collected and published as *An Introduction to Ritual Magic*[4].

Reincarnation and Karma

Lucas' inhuman impersonality crumbles as he begins to develop tender feelings towards the girl he is so ruthlessly using. This marks an important stage in his development as a human being, which has been aborted rather than developed through his misunderstanding of initiation. The true initiate should express and experience life more abundantly rather than suppressing part of himself.

Dion Fortune underpins this important realisation with the theory of the evolution of consciousness, in which she cites two basic methods of raising occult power. One method being to place oneself in the vanguard of spiritual evolution, and the other being to retreat to its rear. The first way, that of the right-hand path, involves high ideals and dedication to selfless service to others, the second, that of the left-hand path, involves a complete withdrawal from human commitments.

This latter way leads to a solitary, self centred, asocial life, free from any sense of moral obligation to anyone, and in its extreme expression divorced from any scruples or remorse. As she puts it, "the occultist of the left-hand path can only glow in a moral vacuum." Occult power is available because it is not bound up in emotional or intellectual intercourse.

However, Lucas' soul, up until now hermetically sealed by his self-imposed false form of training, has been caught by

---

[4] *An Introduction to Ritual Magic* (Thoth Publications, 1997)

Veronica's natural charm and innocence. On the day, on an impulse of compassion, he hands the key of the gardens to Veronica, he has for the first time since boyhood had a thought that did not centre about his own ego. Before he knows where he is, instead of treating her with as little objective concern as a telephone, he is trying to explain to her something of what he is doing, seeking to gain her voluntary co-operation and approval.

This is a reversal of their former positions. Lucas the aloof, Lucas the autocrat, is pleading for something that is within her power to give or to withhold. Yet his concerns still coalesce around visions of personal power, albeit now couched, for Veronica's benefit, in terms of universal philanthropy. However, this self serving hypocrisy does not get past Veronica's natural intuition.

He begins to realise how lonely he is upon his chosen path, and to fantasise about working with her occultly as a priest and priestess of the nature forces, and in a passage in evocation of Pan, Dion Fortune anticipates something of her later novel, *The Goat-Foot God*.

He then reverts to trying to force his view upon her with hypnotic force, yet although at first her passive psychism causes her to succumb, with a gasp she suddenly returns to normal consciousness, to find Lucas standing before her, grey faced and profusely sweating, staggering away as if he has received a great shock. Recovering himself, he says that he had not realised that she was "under protection".

This is apparently because, as she began to sink under Lucas' hypnotic control, her thoughts wandered to a childhood prayer. We might indeed surmise that it was the same protective power that she had met in trance that caused her mind to move in this direction. At any rate, she has formed a link in faith with the Divine that closes a spiritual circuit that causes Lucas to be thrown off forcibly with considerable shock.

This shock sets Lucas thinking, and leads him to conclude that they must have been closely linked in a previous life. The scenario that comes to mind is of their being cousins in ancient Rome, betrothed to each other at a tender age. He leaves for a while to become an initiate of the pagan Mysteries at Eleusis, only to find when he returns that she has become a Christian, who refuses to marry him. Through this rejection, he turned to evil magic, and his view is that although as a Christian she may have saved many souls, by her rejection of him she had caused him to lose his. Therefore, in the way that esoteric theory is often twisted to serve the interests of those who invoke it, he announces "You owe me a debt, Veronica."

In Lucas' ruminations upon the relationship between them, we can see evidence of Jungian thought being considered by Dion Fortune at this time. He does not question her too deeply because he considers she could not put her thoughts into words, being "of the feeling type, not the reasoning type."

He is still puzzled about the shock he has experienced when trying to make her completely subject to his will, while recognising it as "one of the rushes of unseen force with which those who traffic in occult things are familiar." And he begins to wonder if it was something other than his own intuitive powers that caused him to pick out Veronica from a roomful of women at the secretarial agency.

Whilst claiming great importance for the theory of reincarnation as a contribution to western thought Dion Fortune was well aware of its possible abuses. It is a simple matter to construct elaborate romances of wish fulfilment and pass them off as psychic perceptions or ancient memories. Such fantasies rise frequently in the circumstances of illicit romance.

However, in the situation in which Lucas and Veronica find themselves, these motives appear not to pertain. Lucas, as he vaguely recalls the white villa of Roman times containing the gentle girl, and beyond that to other lives as priest and priestess together, right back to "the dim dawn of knowledge in the sun-worship of ancient Atlantis," might well be manufacturing romantic wish fulfilment dreams that derive from his self imposed emotional starvation, but in the circumstances they do tend to lead to his moral regeneration and to abort his selfish plans. Veronica remains largely a passive and innocent party through all of this, having no esoteric theories to cloud the issue, and in this lies her eventual dominance and strength.

Nonetheless the images described by him strike some kind of chord within her, which suggests that possibly they may be recovering the fragments of ancient memories. Although the story he has told her is relatively trite it does not simply disappear but begins to conjure persistent images within her mind. Not only of the white villa, but of sub-tropical gardens, oxen at the well wheel, and slaves tilling the vine terraces. She also has an emotional reaction to the story, and feels she wants to justify the ancient girl for refusing her lover. What else could she have done, when their lives were plainly going in different directions?

She turns spontaneously to Lucas and asks a question that is fermenting in her mind. What was the young Roman's name? He answers equally spontaneously, that it was Justinian – whilst she had the same name as now, Veronica. This seems to be a favoured theory of Dion Fortune - that subsequent lives may carry the same or a similar name.

Lucas is fairly well satisfied with the results of their conversation about previous incarnations. He has deliberately engineered it to some degree, but it also marks the beginning of a profound change in their relationship, although he does not yet foresee the consequences that may arise from this. On the contrary, realising that a greater complexity has entered his plans, especially if old karmic ties are reactivated, he decides to press on quickly with his nefarious plans as quickly as he can. This of course only serves to precipitate the crisis that will result in his spiritual realignment.

In all his attempts to explain to Veronica some of the deeper implications of occult power, and to justify his way to its attainment, he has been undermined by her simple argument of asking what his ultimate aim might be. If there are forces upon another plane that cause things to happen on this one, she asks, what does he wish to do once he has gained control of that plane of causation.

It is only in the depths of despair following his aborted plans that he begins to realise that power exercised from a selfish motivation has a certain hollowness. Isolation might bring power, but it is only in co-operation that happiness lies, and that can only come through love.

Occult Techniques and Technicalities

At the time when Dion Fortune was writing these early works various techniques such as hypnosis and the projection of consciousness in a subtle body were taken a great deal more seriously than they tend to be nowadays. Much of the atmosphere of secrecy that pervaded esoteric circles in those days derived from a fear of what abuses might be unleashed by unscrupulous use of these powers, fears which, for one reason or another, were largely exaggerated.

On the other hand, much knowledge about such techniques had fallen into the discard during the nineteenth century when "mesmerism" and concepts such as "odic force" and "animal magnetism" had been discredited, perhaps a little facilely and prematurely. Dion Fortune began to take account of these levels some years later, as a result of studying some oriental texts on yoga together with a closer acquaintance with the activities of more responsible spiritualist circles. This resulted in her writing a series of articles in which she writes of an amalgam of these matters in terms of "the lost secrets of western occultism." These appeared in the *Inner Light Magazine* in 1939/40, as *The Circuit of Force*, which has since been published in volume form[5] with some additional material culled by myself from 19th century French sources where a great deal of experimentation along these lines went on, long after they were abandoned by the English speaking world.

We can tell where Dion Fortune is coming from at the time of writing *The Demon Lover*, for in another series of articles she wrote in 1929/30, *The Literature of Illuminism*, she lists the esoteric books that have impressed her most. These have also been republished as part of *Practical Occultism.*[6] (Thoth Publications, 2002).

Her eclectic approach to occultism is revealed by the fact that in a review of books on Hatha Yoga she cites Muldoon and Carrington's *Projection of the Astral Body*, along with Kilner's *The Human Aura* and Baudouin's *Suggestion and Auto-suggestion*. She was also familiar with Theosophical works collated by A.E.Powell in *The Etheric Double* and *The Astral Body* as well as *The Causal Body*, and texts closer to the native eastern traditions such as *The Serpent Power* and *Principles of Tantra* by Arthur Avalon (Sir John Woodruffe). Oddly enough, Muldoon and Carrington's *Projection of the Astral Body* also merits a mention at the foot of her review of books on Witchcraft.

Sylvan Muldoon's remarkable experiences of being consciously projected from the physical body were written up in conjunction with the psychical researcher Hereward Carrington. It becomes clear that it is a somewhat rare gift, if gift it can be called, for Muldoon is obviously a man in poor health and with a not entirely well balanced endocrine system. Added to which, his projections were first produced by a severe electric shock from a fallen power cable. Thus not a technique that budding occultists are advised to try at home!

---

[5] *The Circuit of Force* (Thoth Publications, 1998)
[6] *Practical Occultism* (Thoth Publications, 2002).

There is thus a wide gap between what might better be called "etheric projection" of the kind experienced by Sylvan Muldoon and certain rare individuals, largely as a result of genetic make-up or abnormal circumstances, (including near-death experiences), and the concentrated use of the imagination which may or may not develop into complete lack of awareness of the sensations of the physical body. It is this which is more likely to be what is meant by the term "astral projection" and although there were certain, somewhat cumbersome, techniques in the Golden Dawn system for trying to project consciousness into a deliberately built up "imaginal" body, this seems to be by no means essential in order to gain the benefits of creative visualisation of symbolic scenarios as a gateway to higher consciousness.

Such techniques have become relatively commonplace in various forms of therapy and creative development nowadays, even in quite orthodox circles. The fact that it is the imagination that is being used does not mean that it is merely evanescent fantasy. The imagination is a very important tool of the human psyche, and can also be a fearsome task master – in extreme cases giving substance to various forms of prejudice and obsessive behaviour in a grim scale that leads all the way to insanity.

There is a close connection between occultism and psychology although they should not be confused, despite each being able to throw some light upon the other discipline. Dion Fortune abandoned psychotherapy in favour of occultism in 1916, although she always maintained a keen interest in it. Throughout the time of writing her novels she was in correspondence with Olga Fróbe-Kapteyn, founder of the famous Jungian Eranos Institute in Switzerland. It was part of her belief that anyone aspiring to become a true initiate must needs be psychologically well balanced, if necessary through some form of psychotherapy. However occultism took over from where psychology left off.

Part of the change that can be seen between her approach of the 1920's and that of the 1930's is that in the former she tends to be explaining occultism in terms of psychology whilst in the latter she is explaining psychology in terms of occultism. She has passed, through personal experience, a great divide.

Part Two

The Mysteries of the Sun and the Earth

Chapter Three
The Winged Bull

The Story

The time is the early 1930's and 33 year old Ted Murchison, who went straight from school to serve as a junior officer in the trenches in the First World War, is still finding it difficult to settle down to civilian life, and has drifted through a number of dead end jobs. As the novel opens he is spending a foggy Sunday afternoon killing time at the British Museum.

He has been somewhat exasperated by the official guide, "patronising both the dead and the living" but is considerably impressed by some of the artefacts, notably in the Egyptian Gallery and more specifically by one of the great Assyrian winged bulls (although erroneously called Babylonian in the novel). Reflecting upon his current frustrations with modern life he is moved by the atmosphere of the museum to make a spontaneous invocation to the ancient gods as he emerges into the fog outside, and immediately and fortuitously runs into his former commanding officer in the army, Colonel Alick Brangwyn, who had been almost a father figure to him during the war.

In the course of conversation it appears that they could be mutually helpful to one another and Brangwyn offers Ted a temporary post as his general secretary/chauffeur, living in at his maisonette in Bloomsbury. However the job that Brangwyn really has in mind is more in the nature of a minder for Ursula, his pretty 28 year old half-sister, who has become involved with some undesirable characters on the occult scene. Not that her involvement with the occult is, in itself, of any great concern to Brangwyn, for he is something of an adept himself.

Murchison is completely ignorant of such matters but soon finds himself embarked on a steep learning curve as he becomes involved with Ursula and her problems. The occult scenario is at first presented to him as some form of psychological experiment, to assist in which he is advised to read up on mythology and to keep a record of his dreams which he is to discuss freely with his new employer.

The more serious side to the problem becomes apparent when Frank Fouldes, Ursula's former fiancé, turns up unexpectedly with his sinister and seedy mentor Hugo Astley. It becomes apparent that Ursula is easily thrown into a fascinated hypnotic state against her will and by these means they seek to draw her more closely into their ambit for their own insalubrious sexual and occult purposes. No match for them in terms of occult knowledge or power Ted Murchison deals with them effectively by the simple expedient of throwing them downstairs.

Forced to keep their physical distance Fouldes and Astley resort to telepathic assault as a consequence of which Ted finds himself drawn into a strange battle of wills with unseen forces. All this is somewhat beyond his understanding but he manages as best he can, and is temporarily successful for the attack is diverted from Ursula onto himself, at little more cost than leaving him drained of vital energy. This provides an opportunity for Ursula, encouraged by Colonel Brangwyn, to restore him to normality by a practical demonstration of a contrasexual exchange of polar magnetism.

The couple now begin to realise Brangwyn's ulterior motive in hiring Ted, which goes further than his simply being a minder for Ursula, but as a possible emotional replacement for her former fiancé Frank Fouldes. Baldly expressed, the word 'gigolo' comes readily to their minds; it is a situation that, understandably, neither of them finds particularly attractive.

In many ways they are opposite types. Ted is Nordic, extraverted and socially gauche, whilst Ursula is Celtic, introverted, and socially sophisticated. Nonetheless Brangwyn insists that to avoid Ursula suffering from a relapse, there is no alternative but to continue with the arrangement for the time being. What is more, he thinks a small experiment in ceremonial magic might help to resolve the situation. This they prepare to enact.

The ritual is fairly simple and largely spontaneous, accompanied by music and with words taken from the poetry of Swinburne. Broadly speaking it involves Murchison identifying himself with the Sun god, and Ursula with the Earth goddess. The symbolic underpinning is provided in a quotation given by Dion Fortune at the beginning of the book, from the poetry of William Watson:

> For of old the Sun, our sire,
> Came wooing the mother of men,
> Earth, that was virginal then,
> Vestal fire to his fire.
> Silent her bosom and coy,
> But the strong god sued and pressed;
> And born of their starry nuptial joy
> Are all that drink of her breast.

Immediately after this ritual Brangwyn despatches Ursula to a favourite *pied á terre* of hers in North Wales, in the hope that the effect of the ceremony will continue to work away in the subconscious minds of the celebrants, undisturbed by superficial personality clashes. At the same time it provides him with the chance to give Murchison some more specific occult training and instruction.

In the meantime Astley gingerly approaches Ted Murchison, other methods having failed, in the hope of bribing him to betray Brangwyn. Ted pretends to go along with this suggestion and discovers that Astley who already has a close neighbour acting as a spy for him, knows full well where Ursula has gone and has sent Fouldes after her.

Alarmed at Ursula's vulnerability Murchison and Brangwyn set off urgently by car for Snowdonia. They find that Fouldes has already confronted Ursula but been aborted by the intervention of the farm dogs who came to her protection. However Ursula admits that she might well have gone with Fouldes if the dogs had not driven him off.

The ritual seems to have had some effect, for Ted and Ursula are beginning to become more attracted to one another, although their time together is beset by a series of minor irritations and misunderstandings. In the end, after a further confrontation with Fouldes, in which honours remain about even, they return to London and the possibility of working another ritual.

Before this can occur however, Ursula, walking out alone one day is accosted by Hugo Astley, and by a combination of duplicitous persuasion and light hypnosis is taken back to his house. Ted thereupon goes off in search of Astley to pose as a bribable accomplice.

He discovers that Astley is planning an obscene ritual in which Ursula will take the part of the virgin upon the altar, with Fouldes playing the part of the bull in a reconstruction of the legend of Pasiphae. Ted is invited to take part and is set to build some of the temple furniture for the rite. He finds a chance to speak with Ursula before the event but, still dominated by Fouldes and Astley, she is determined to stay. After Ted's departure she changes her mind, but it is too late, for Astley forcibly prevents her from leaving.

Despite the possible danger to himself, Ted turns up to take part in Astley's ritual and succeeds in disrupting it, before in typical strong arm fashion he takes Ursula away, giving Fouldes a severe thrashing on the way.

His relationship with Ursula still unresolved, Ted decides to cut his emotional losses and seek a job overseas. However, the inveterate matchmaker Brangwyn arranges for the two of them to meet up again unexpectedly at a little cottage on the Yorkshire coast. Here, left to themselves, explanations as to all misunderstandings ensue, they plight their troth and true love blossoms with full expectation of imminent wedding bells.

*   *   *

In her new series of novels Dion Fortune claimed that nothing she wrote was fortuitous, everything was there for a reason, albeit a subconscious reason, for she wrote very much in the vein of free fantasy, off her own subconscious. Since writing her earlier fiction she had certainly matured a great deal esoterically, not least through writing *The Mystical Qabalah* from which the later novels can be said to derive. They give her understanding of the practical application of certain Qabalistic principles in the actions and experiences of the characters.

When Ted Murchison finds himself in a fog in the opening scene of *The Winged Bull* it is not there simply for atmospheric effect. It represents his own confused state of mind, uncertain of which way to go. But apart from this symbolic element the fog also has an effect upon his consciousness, for the sensory deprivation that is induced by fog, particularly the very dense ones once experienced by Londoners, is to open up the psychic faculties. These have already been stimulated by his wandering around amongst the old gods of the British Museum, sensitised by the magnetism that the various artefacts and galleries give off.

He has been particularly impressed by the great winged bulls from Assyria that flank the doorway, and they are also to stand at the doorway of his own entry upon the path of initiation. His inner senses are further heightened by a great disappointment he has just received in being turned down yet again in his search for a job, and heightened emotion plus symbolic imagery of the ancient pantheons is the very stuff of magic, whether he realises it or not.

Consequently he is impelled, on an irrational impulse, to cry "Io Pan! Io Pan!" as he emerges into the fog outside, and to his surprise his call is immediately answered, in the form of his old commanding officer, an occultist of some advancement to boot. This may seem to stretch the arm of coincidence rather far, but however convenient this may seem for the writer of fiction, such chance happenings, or "signs following", are by no means unknown to those who are familiar with the deeper reaches of occultism, which contact the levels of causation beyond the plane of physical effects.

The consequence of his invocation is to find him a job, as he sought. It also releases him from the constricting atmosphere of the relatives with whom he lives, and introduces him to the entourage of an occult teacher. He is thus now set upon a path of initiation.

The situation in which he finds himself is, at the most basic level, that of a hero protecting a maiden in distress from designs of evil men who seek to capture and abuse her. This is not just the work of a physical minder or even of coping with the forces of misapplied magic. It goes beyond that to winning the confidence and then the heart of the maiden in question, in a potential union of opposites, overcoming her own prejudices towards him and his own prejudices against her.

They are of opposing types in a number of ways, including their ancestral heritage, which mirrors a deep divide in the history of the nation itself. In legendary terms it goes back to the battle of the Red Dragon against the White, the Celt against Saxon, overtones of other periods as in Alfred's West Saxons against the Danes, or at a later period as the strife of the Wars of the Roses, of the red of Lancaster against the white of York. In more remote periods there would have been the conflict between the indigenous Bronze age peoples and the invading iron age Celts.

This is not quite so far fetched as it might seem, for one of the elements of the deeper side of occultism concerns what might be termed the complexes or even pathologies of the group soul of the nation at large. And by nation one means no narrow racial identification but the consciousness of all tribes, individuals or extended families, that have chosen to live their life within these shores. They become, in effect, the consciousness of the land which they inhabit. And over time it is the land which will affect the way they think and act.

So in the reconciliation of Ted Murchison and Ursula Brangwyn we see, at one level, a talismanic reconciliation of deep divisions within the land and the nation.

There is a higher union still beyond this, as is evident in the ritual that Brangwyn conceives for the two of them – one as the Sun Hero and the other as the Earth Maiden, in the poem that we have already quoted.

Murchison is instructed in the techniques of ceremonial magic by the use of music and dance, which although perhaps not a comprehensive introduction to the discipline is perhaps appropriate in this instance.

It is interesting to note that although music is desirable Brangwyn eschews the use of a gramophone because "there's no life about it." Much the same could still be said in an era of hi-fidelity reproduction, the use of canned music remains inferior to that of a live instrument – as long of course as it is competently played. But virtuoso performance is not required, simply music played within the technical accomplishments of the musician, and as with the words of any ritual, coming from the heart. We may therefore assume that Brangwyn's violin playing is somewhat beyond the out of tune scraping of a complete beginner. The dancing that goes with it, along with the music, is however very much in the role of a preliminary ice breaker, with the sequence of moods chosen and exploited by the fiddler. A slight magical element is noticeable in his instruction not to reverse in the steps of the old fashioned waltz, presumably the injunction to continue the invoking clockwise direction of movement as observed in the occult lodge.

From this initiation of the emotions they pass naturally to more formal instruction via the pictorial imagination, as Brangwyn brings out paintings depicting evocative scenes of temples in ancient Egypt, and beyond that to evocations of ancient lost civilisations such as the mythical Atlantis.

In the ritual which they eventually perform Merchison, representing the Sun, is clad in a gold robe upon which is emblazoned a golden rayed sun disc whilst Ursula as the Earth is in a filmy green robe. The temple in which they work is entirely of gold and when Brangwyn appears, as its heirophant, he is robed in pink and gold, the colours of Tiphareth, the sphere of the Sun on the Tree of Life, and wears a headdress of the two lands of Egypt, which signifies the outer and the inner worlds.

Brangwyn's prior instructions, short and to the point, are worth being taken to heart by any intending practitioners of the ceremonial art. His music and chanting, he tells them, if he does his part properly, ought to cause images to rise in their imagination, for that is the aim of it – to stir the imagination. To accept these images as if they were real. It is a form of imagination of which the academic schools know nothing for it requires whole hearted participation to realise its effectiveness. But they will certainly know something about it before they are finished, and see how extraordinarily effectual it is.

In this sequence and all that follows, despite the fact that in the circumstances of the novel it may give the impression of being no more than a somewhat odd private "tea dance", so popular in those days, Dion Fortune give us a unique exposition of some of the techniques of a magical ritual, together with a run down of some of the subjective reactions of someone taking part in one. This is a quite remarkable revelation, bearing in mind the time of writing, when all such matters were held in the strictest secrecy. However Dion Fortune obviously felt that the veil of the temple could safely and helpfully be raised under the guise of fiction.

Just prior to the commencement of the ritual we are treated to a description of the subjective reactions of Murchison, coming to this kind of thing for the first time. He finds a certain swinging between inner and outer consciousness, as at first he simply observes physically what is about him. This gives him an opportunity to regard Ursula at length, for she is sitting opposite him, with eyes closed. She has a certain beauty about her that he finds attractive, calling to his mind an image of the lover of a hero, Lady Hamilton, the mistress of Lord Nelson. This gives way to consideration of Ursula's aloof fastidiousness which is written in every line of her body and he experiences a feeling of rejection, then of pity for the man who might marry her, leading to a sudden dislike for her, as something male within him resents her atmosphere of virginal untouchability.

In a sudden surge of satiric mirth and mischief he wonders what it would be like to knock her off her pedestal and roll her in the earth. For a moment he identifies with the figure of a goat god chasing a nymph. Then he pulls himself together and recalls who he is and that he is in the company of his employer and his employer's sister. Immediately the glamour of the temple furnishings fall away from his gaze and he sees them merely as painted plywood and curtains bought from drapery stores, the golden thrones as gilded chairs from cheap antique shops. This mood as quickly passes as he looks at Ursula again, thinking she looks tense and apprehensive, and the goat mood gives way to a feeling of sympathy for a fellow human being. He is then startled by a clear bell like note that rings through the temple from behind the east and the resonant voice of the magus, Brangwyn, calling the temple to order. It is the traditional cry of the Dionysiac mysteries, warning the profane to fly from the path of the divinely inspired worshippers lest they be torn to pieces by their frenzy. With this comes a frisson of fear, which can be the surest presage of a successful psychic experiment.

The sound of the violin is evocative of the elements, at first like rippling water, then of the wind in spring woods that are in bare leaf, then deepening to evoke the summer woods in deep leaf and full of bird song, and finally rushing, circling fire music that makes him think of the sun's corona with its towering flames licking thousands of miles in height. The magus then enters and calls the two of them to their feet where they stand, Ursula almost in a sleep walking hypnoidal state it would appear, while the Swinburnian evocation is chanted, and it should be said that there is a great deal of difference between poetry chanted aloud and simply reading it silently off the page.

All begins with a sense of desolation at a world deserted by its God. Then Murchison, feeling the misery and frustration of the world flowing over him begins to feel an actual part of it, rather than reacting to it with a personal depression, as the ritual tells of a dying god. Following from this come to mind thoughts of the great pagan Roman emperor, Julian the Apostate, as a note of furtive triumph creeps into the words and music as if the waking of the old gods were taking place to break through the repressions of medieval piety. Who is this unnamed god who is being evoked, whose power he feels beginning to fill the room?

There flickers before his inward vision a landscape like the surface of the moon, and in the centre of it, Saturn the oldest of the Olympean gods. Then comes a moment of revelation as he suddenly realises the faith for which he has been searching, in the one great Creator and Sustainer of the Universe, whose form changes as the powers of mankind's understanding increase. The real Being behind all gods. A God who was so many-sided that no one could see every side at once. There was a Christian facet, an Old Testament facet, a Hindu facet, a Taoist facet, many pagan facets – a God as many-sided as the soul of man.

With his realisation of the One God being behind all manifestations of him dreamed of by the mind of man, Murchison begins to wonder which facet will be the object of the continuing evocation, and then he realises it is an invocation to the sun god, hence this golden temple and his golden robes.

The rest of the ceremony is driven by music rather than words, first Dionysian gypsy tunes and syncopated rhythms that stir the blood, which give way to ancient chant forms that have a strange effect upon him. He feels as if a vast pair of hawk's wings were overshadowing him, along with a curious warm glow that seems to envelop him, and then he suddenly finds voice, spontaneously crying out "Ra! Ra! Ra!" – the name of the ancient Egyptian god. Feeling a kind of humming gathering strength in his throat he realises that some form of mediumship or spontaneous creativity is overtaking him as he breaks forth with: "I am Horus, god of the morning; I mount the sky on eagle's wings. I am Ra in mid-heaven; I am the sun in splendour. I am Toum of the downsetting. I am also Kephra at midnight. Thus spake the priest with the mask of Osiris."

The rest of the rite is largely expunged from his memory, as it takes place in a state of higher consciousness. He dimly recalls a slow hieratic dance together with the priestess and going to the altar at the western side of the temple where they drink together from a cup of wine, eat of broken bread dipped into salt, and inhale the fragrance of the pine branches and cones that are laid there.

This, however, is simply the outward show upon the physical plane. Upon the higher levels they are not two individuals but two great forces. He is the sun in heaven bringing life to the earth. She is the earth, absorbing it hungrily, drawing it from him to satisfy her crying needs. And the more she draws from him, the more flows into him. He feels himself all brightness, as if he were compact of shining gold. And he feels the woman in his arms gradually light up like the earth at dawn as the sun steals over the line of the eastern hills. Finally she, too, is all brightness, and they are made as one as they circle in the slow rhythm round the temple. Then twilight begins to fall, the music moves slower, and finally there is silence. Together they stand before the altar with its pine boughs, its bread, wine and salt. Hands of blessing are extended over them, and consciousness returns to normal.

As Brangwyn has stated beforehand, this was not a set ritual in which the officers recite written parts, but a spontaneous one in which Brangwyn, with the general plan in his head, directs the operation, whilst the others do whatever occurs to them spontaneously. He explains it as a kind of acted psychoanalysis, enabling the subconscious mind to come up to the surface, to which he adds "and there are some strange powers in the subconsciousness, believe me."

The theological conclusions that Murchison has come to in the course of this rite, virtually an identification of the sun god Apollo with the One Supreme Being of Judeo-Christian belief, have caused Dion Fortune's position to be described as "Anglicanism turned sorcerous and polytheistic". Anglican she certainly was, as may be seen from her *Mystical Meditations upon the Collects* (biblical readings from the Anglican liturgy) and her staunch stand against the orientalisation of Christian belief which caused her to break from the Theosophical Society to found her own school of initiation. She also, in conjunction with her colleague C.T. Loveday, maintained a public form of Christian worship in The Guild of the Master Jesus. Her mystical meditations, it should be said, had a homespun flavour of their own but of their piety and sincerity there can be no doubt.

The charge of sorcery is one to which she would have taken great exception, and in her definition in *The Mystical Qabalah*, white magic "consists in the application of occult powers to spiritual ends" whilst as regards the polytheistic element she goes on to say "The Qabalah is essentially monotheistic; the potencies it classifies are always regarded as the messengers of God and not His fellow-workers." And consequently "the Qabalah supplies the best groundwork and the best system upon which to train a student before he begins to experiment with the pagan systems."

Murchison, it is true, in the somewhat unusual circumstances of the novel, is pitchforked into a pagan system without opportunity for very much Qabalistic preparation, but it is these principles that provide the hidden structure for this and the subsequent novels. Perhaps another useful insight into Dion Fortune's attitude in these matters is provided in a little ceremony which she wrote for the consecration of her sanctuary at Chalice Orchard, Glastonbury in 1932:

> *"Let us adore the Ancient Ones that we may be known of them and They may bless us in the sowing, in the reaping and in the baking; in the hearth fire, in the rooftree and in the byre, in the bed and at board; in the fighting and in the feasting. For Adonai is the Lord of the Kingdom of Earth. All things earthly are holy unto Him and the Gods of old time are His Voices. Blessed are those mighty Ones who speak with the Voice of Adonai; may we hear them with inner ear and see them with the inner eye, and be blessed of Them in all that we do in the Kingdom of Nature."*

Central to the pagan godforms evoked in this novel is the Assyrian Winged Bull, which, it should be said, also plays a major role in Christo-Judaic iconography as one of the Holy Living Creatures before the Throne of God. For the purposes of the novel, however, it carries a more psychological significance, although not without theological overtones. It represents the instinctual drives of man raised up upon spiritual wings, and the spiritual side of man united with the instinctual, via human experience and intelligence. This is later expressed in the initiatory rubric "Bring the Godhead down into manhood, and take manhood up into Godhead."

This has been a lesson that Alick Brangwyn has previously been trying to instil into the somewhat refined, and even prissy, Ursula, with Frank Fouldes in mind as a suitable partner for her. He had been given the guardianship of Ursula when she was still a seventeen year old at convent school with ambitions to become a nun. A milieu from which he immediately removed her in the opinion that convent teaching was all wrong about sex. Up until then, Ursula confesses, it had been ground into her that sex was coarse and vulgar and evil. Contemporary attitudes towards this, in the social ambience of seventy years ago, was a major concern of Dion Fortune, and nor was she by any means alone in this. She simply had her own ways of going about it.

Not that all has been plain sailing in Alick Brangwyn's course of action, for Frank Fouldes has proved to be something of a broken reed. Although he had shown much promise under Brangwyn's esoteric instruction, he was an easily influenced and impatient young man, who because he felt he was not making sufficiently rapid progress, turned to other teachers, and disastrously to the notorious Hugo Astley. Here we are shown the averse side of the occult world and in a singularly literal way, for Astley has a ritual of his own, based upon the symbolism of the bull, and it is one of degradation of the spirit.

In plain terms it is a reconstruction of the myth of Pasiphae, whose depraved lust caused her to wish to be coupled to a bull – the result of which was the monstrous minotaur – the ravening beast in the labyrinth. In this re-enactment Ursula is to take the place of Pasiphae, in a particular interpretation of the classic black magic scenario of the naked virgin upon the altar, whilst the rather unlikely Fouldes will play the part of the bull. With a particularly blasphemous slant all this will be enacted under the gaze of the crucified saviour, a part which

Astley has reserved for Ted Murchison. A full realisation of the implications of all this may have been the cause of one reader to have thrown the book across the room in horror, rather than a stimulation of repressed complexes.

The iniquities of this scenario speak for themselves, and show the depths to which an occultist of the left hand path can sink. One may well however, cast a critical eye upon Alick Brangwyn's performance as an adept of the right hand path, for it is a consequence, at least in part, of his own mismanagement and manipulation of others' lives that Ursula is in her current difficulties. The worst that the convent had to offer might well have been preferable to all this!

In a series of three articles in *The Inner Light Magazine* towards the end of 1937 Dion Fortune took up this very point. It might well be said, she admitted, that Brangwyn was lacking in shrewdness in failing to detect Fouldes' weaknesses, but there are easily overlooked circumstances which explain why this should be so. When Fouldes was in the presence of Brangwyn his weaker side was not to be seen, for an adept develops pupils by calling out their higher side and making it function — an entirely unconscious process because it is a consequence not of what the adept does but of what he is. Conversely, the reason Fouldes went to the bad was for much the same reason that Brangwyn made an error of judgement about him, the hyper-suggestibility of the psychic type, which laid him open to the evil influence of Astley. This was exacerbated by the fact that Brangwyn was well able to judge Fouldes' rate of progress upon the initiatory path and to withhold from him that for which he was not yet ready. This incensed Fouldes and sent him off to investigate other teachers, including Astley, which proved to be his undoing.

She also makes the point that because Brangwyn is an adept does not mean to say that he is perfect; he may have considerable knowledge but he is not perfect in wisdom. Of course, had he been so, she also points out, there would have been no effective story for her to write!

Brangwyn has a penchant for the finer things in life that verges on the fastidious, from silken dressing gowns to stone-ground porridge, as part of an ideal of healthy and hygienic living, although his taste for tobacco might seem at variance with this, although the health hazards of nicotine were generally not realised in his day.

Some of the views he expresses on genetic engineering might seem a little disquieting, particularly in the light of what was currently going on along these lines in Nazi Germany at the time. However his remarks seem more generally speculative in reference to pre-history and legends of the lost continent of Atlantis than any proposed programme for modern racial purity. As Murchison points out, there is already a certain genetic selection that goes on, determined by inherited wealth. The general concensus of the conversation is that such methods, whatever might have been the practice in ancient times, would nowadays be unworkable, whilst Murchison has a distinctly unflattering view of Adolf Hitler together, it must be said, with a similar view of the German people for electing him.

This is in the context of a short piece of exposition on the doctrine of the group or racial soul, a concept with which Dion Fortune was much taken, partly as a result of reading *Instincts of the Herd in Peace and War*, a sociological and psychological treatise by Wilfred Trotter FRS, which became popular immediately after the First World War for its comparison between British and German national characteristics.

In practical terms this is the cue for a further lesson in levels of consciousness from Brangwyn. Murchison, he suggests felt the British group soul when he went over the top out of the trenches. As one berserk, like his Viking ancestors, he felt a tremendous pressure of life within him, as if he could have gone through anything, even a brick wall, in a sense of invulnerability which even communicated itself to those who served under him. It was a kind of "divine inebriation", and Brangwyn explains that there are similar types of pressure that may be experienced under the spell of religious experience or of falling in love. Whilst magic is a way of inducing this kind of supra-personal consciousness at will.

Murchison's magical instruction is both practical and theoretical, and helps to serve one purpose of the book, as an instructional primer for the discerning occult student. In part this is the advice to read up on certain subjects such as myth and legend and to instil the mind with certain pictures of antiquity. It also involves a certain analysis of dreams, one of which is a prevision of Ursula's face, whilst other dreams cast her in various guises as black Persian cat or black stallion, reminders of her raven hair.

This is no more than fairly conventional psychology that Brangwyn is using as a diagnostic indicator to the progress of his plans as reflected in Murchison's subconscious mind. Beyond this, however, is the experience of the exchange of animal magnetism.

This is demonstrated in two ways. One is the way in which Ursula can be completely dominated by someone such as Fouldes or Astley, having already once fallen under their influence voluntarily. Another is the way that this seems to be capable of being transmitted over a distance, in what is the last instance we find in Dion Fortune's fiction of this kind of occult skulduggery, which is as rare as it is difficult to perform, as Dr. Taverner has previously observed.

The third instance of the exchange of animal magnetism is an entirely therapeutic one in the recharging of Murchison's energies by Ursula after he has been vitally drained in protecting her from psychic attack. As described in the novel the technique seems one of simplicity itself, as Murchison is instructed to stand with the palms of his hands placed against hers and to enter into the spirit of the thing imaginatively.

However, at first this is a failure because the conditions are not right, neither of them being in a sufficiently relaxed and sympathetic emotional rapport.

Once this initial problem is overcome however, and Murchison has no need to be told to enter the experiment imaginatively, as Ursula's feelings are evidently deeply stirred these in turn affect his own. He feels her hands trembling slightly as she places the palms hard against his own but instead of being cold, as they had been before, they now burn with a kind of dry electric heat as if conducting an electric current. Everything else fades from his consciousness as her eyes are fixed upon his and he feels a glowing warmth spreading all over him until at last, the charging complete, he comes back to himself standing before the flushed and smiling girl, knowing that something very definite has been done to him, although he does not know what. However, it has restored him to normal and he no longer feels terribly drained, as he had done before.

Much of the theory of this was being investigated by Dion Fortune at the time of writing her novels and she later went on to write a series of articles in *The Inner Light Magazine*, from February 1939 to August 1940, in which she called them part of "the lost secrets of the West". These articles have now been republished, in volume form, under their original title *The Circuit of Force*[1] with a commentary providing the gist of much of her background reading together with material from 19th century French sources, which took the theory and practice of animal magnetism rather more seriously than did the Anglo-Saxon world.

We find also in *The Winged Bull* a broader treatment of the subject of etheric magnetism in the different localities. As Dion Fortune later wrote in her notes upon the novel, she feels strongly about localities, and they were not chosen at random in her book, but provide an appropriate background for the

---
[1] *The Circuit of Force*, Thoth Publications, 1998

action that is taking place. To a sensitive, she points out, all places, have definite psychic characteristics. Thus we have in the novel the London districts of Bloomsbury and Acton, and an undisclosed area of north-east London, together with the country locales of Snowdonia and the coast of Yorkshire.

The slightly raffish and cosmopolitan area of Bloomsbury is where the main action takes place, in Brangwyn's appartment, fairly free from average Anglo-Saxon repressions, and housing within its midst the old gods contained in the British Museum, where indeed the action commences. The outlying district of Acton, where Murchison is an unwilling lodger with his dreadful relations she associates with the deadness of suburban life, (although with no greater objective justification than having once had some clothes torn by a laundry there – but on such slender associations can the creative imagination thrive!) Whilst the unnamed district that seems to be in the general region of the Hackney marshes is where she sites Astley's noisome abode.

Snowdonia was a natural choice for a power centre in sympathy with Ursula's Celtic origins, whilst the Yorkshire coast is more in keeping with Murchison's Nordic ones. The contrast between these two main characters is thus carried through into the character of the land and of their ancestral origins. Dion Fortune expands somewhat upon this theme in her article.

The Celtic Ursula, she says, is contrasted with the Norse Murchison, upon which turns much of the inner magic of the book. Between them they hold both major lines of inner contact that are available in these islands. Contacts, she says, are a matter of both race and racial tradition, and it is not easy to pick up contacts for which one does not have a natural affinity. This should not be regarded as a brief for any thesis of racial purity, but it is a matter of observable fact that a person with any trace of Welsh, Cornish or Irish blood in their genetic heritage can pick up any of the Celtic contacts more readily, including the Breton ones and the Highland Scottish. On the other hand a person whose roots lie in the eastern side of England, of the Anglo-Saxon and the Dane, will more easily pick up on the Norse and Scandinavian gods and also the Slavonic. However, owing to the fact that our culture stems from the Mediterranean and upon classical traditions, most can readily pick up on any of the contacts of Greece, Rome, Egypt or Chaldea, which all interconnect with one another at a certain level.

In the context of the novel therefore, on the flanks of Snowdon Murchison is at a disadvantage because not connected with the natural magnetism of the place, and this is why Brangwyn arranges for them finally to come together in a Nordic hermitage that will aid him in getting onto his own particular contacts. Indeed, as described in the book, as soon as Murchison crosses the river Humber, returning from Wales, he feels as if he has "come into his own". If a line is drawn from St Alden's (or St Alban's) Head in Dorset to Lindisfarne off the coast of Northumberland, all the Celtic contacts are to be found upon one side of it, she believed, and all the Norse contacts on the other.

In a significant few sentences Dion Fortune explains very much the intended denouement of the book "in a place in which Ursula and Murchison shall do the work he intends them to do, and make a magical marriage, he chooses the spot where Murchison, the less experienced of the two, shall have the advantage of the site, because he needs the extra force to bring him up to the necessary magnetic voltage and enable him to balance Ursula; she being highly trained, will be able to adapt herself to the conditions."

So ends a romantic novel to the expectation of its circulating library readers which at the same time a magical treatise for the edification of her esoteric students. These two ends encompassed in the broader perspective of Dion Fortune's social and psychological concerns.

Chapter Four
The Goat-Foot God

The Story

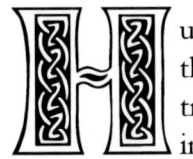

Hugo Paston is a wealthy young man, in his early thirties, who has just suffered a humiliating tragedy. His wife and best friend have been killed in a car crash in circumstances which proves that they were in the midst of a long term adulterous relationship. Wandering distractedly through Bloomsbury, he idly riffles through the bargain bin outside a secondhand bookshop and comes upon an old detective novel by A.E.W. Mason, *The Prisoner in the Opal*.

The title intrigues him, and also the fact that it contains within it the description of a Black Mass. He buys the book and makes the acquaintance of the old bookseller, Jelkes, with whom he strikes up a friendship, and who guides his reading via Huysman's *La Bas* to the more wholesome and instructive fiction of *The Devil's Mistress* by Brodie Innes and *The Corn King and the Spring Queen* by Naomi Mitcheson, and eventually to the descriptions of the ancient mysteries to be found in Iamblichus.

Long conversations with old Jelkes have a therapeutic effect upon Hugh, who has come to realise that up to now he has been valued, not for himself, but for his money. He begins to seek for some deeper meaning to life and to look for experience beyond the superficial existence he has followed up to now. He therefore decides to use his financial resources to seek out direct experience of the Unseen – in ways that somewhat horrify Jelkes, who is much read in these matters, but as the product of a Jesuit seminary, prefers to keep his knowledge on a theoretical plane.

Hugh's first idea is to acquire an old country mansion and to fit up its rooms as separate temples to pagan gods. Seeing that Hugh is firmly committed to this project Jelkes thinks the best he can do is to try to keep a steadying influence on the younger man by cooperating with him to some degree. At the same time it gives him the opportunity to offer a helping hand to Mona Wilton, a young woman towards whom he has a similar avuncular relationship. She is currently having something of a hard time trying to establish herself as an interior designer.

Seeking the location of a suitable building for this unusual project, with the assistance of a study of power centres and ley lines, Hugh lights upon the dilapidated Monks Farm, which turns out to be on the site of a ruined abbey, reputed to be haunted by the ghost of one of the former monks, walled up in medieval times for some serious misdemeanour.

As these arrangements are concluded Hugh begins to have vivid dreams. In one he is running through the countryside of ancient Greece in pursuit of a young girl. In another he is identified with the unfortunate monk Ambrosius, incarcerated for an heretical interest in the ancient Mysteries, and specifically the Rites of Pan.

With the refurbishing of the old farm buildings Hugh becomes more intrigued with these rites and the fate of the medieval monk. This reaches the point where he appears to be overshadowed by the spirit of Ambrosius, an occurrence that so shocks Mona that she suffers a minor breakdown.

As the story develops it becomes difficult to discern the true nature of the situation. Is Ambrosius a ghost haunting the place? Is he a former incarnation of Hugh's? Or is Hugh simply upon the hallucinatory verge of insanity? Or is it a combination of any of these three?

Mona too has her dreams, which correspond to the ancient Greek ones of Hugh, and the two of them begin, at first unconsciously and spontaneously, and then more deliberately, to formulate a Rite of Pan.

In his own way Jelkes comes to his own conclusions about the best way to pull Hugh Paston through this dilemma, by a ritual enactment of his preoccupations. He is apprehensive of the risks that might be involved in this, for he can do little of practical use himself, and the brunt must be borne by Mona Wilton, who by reason of her sex and sympathetic companionship is the one who will trigger these deep seated complexes within Hugh – whether as the nubile young companion of his dreams in ancient Sparta, or the seductive succuba that has troubled the medieval monk. Hugh himself becomes aware of an odd parallel between the fate of the medieval monk and his own condition in modern life, as his family plot to have him certified to be confined in a psychratric hospital.

Meanwhile Mona and Hugh begin to develop a closer rapport with one another, although this is kept on a platonic level because of the wide gap between their social background and temperament. There are however hints of a possible deeper involvement. Mona wonders if indeed there might be a bond between them that was once forged in ancient Greece or whether she is simply the type that appeals to this sex starved male.

Their first attempt at ritual is more in the nature of a psychoanalysis, albeit with the three of them sitting in the temple, with Hugh and Mona clad in appropriate robes. This passes to something less cerebral however when Mona takes up the running, describes some of her own visions, and leads them out onto the greensward where in the moonlight she spontaneously performs what she calls her "moon dance".

Jelkes' worry, and probably not without cause, is that this provocative behaviour on Mona's part may strike so powerfully into Hugh's repressed consciousness that he may run berserk. However, all passes off without major incident, and they move on to a period of psychological speculation as Hugh realises that, whatever its origins, Ambrosius is a repressed part of himself that is striving for outward expression. The question is: who shall be the master in this integration process?

Hugh gradually comes more to terms with the Ambrosius figure, and he begins to wonder how the forces of Pan might be expressed, not in ancient or medieval terms, but in the circumstances of the present day. Fortuitously he comes upon an ancient grove in the pinewoods with a fallen monolith in its centre.

Things fall readily into place from here on. Hugh and Mona resolve their differences and marry, although it is clearly revealed that the more important ceremony takes place not in the local church but in the Rite of Pan that they perform in the ancient grove as the preliminary to their wedding night.

*   *   *

There is a similarity in the relationship of characters in *The Goat-Foot God* and *The Winged Bull*, each concerns the burgeoning relationship of a young man and woman overseen by a senior third party. Colonel Brangwyn played this overseeing role with Ursula and Ted in *The Winged Bull* whilst Jelkes the bookseller does much the same with regard to Hugh and Mona.

There is a considerable contrast between the two male elements in the equation, the fastidious taste and habits of Colonel Brangwyn compare markedly with the rough and ready Ted Murchison, and the scruffy old Jelkes is some distance removed on the social and intellectual scale from the wealthy socialite Hugh Paston.

However, each of the older men exercise an expansive influence and provide a source of instruction for the younger one – almost in the form of an initiator one might say, bearing in mind the esoteric underpinning of the stories involved.

Jelkes and Brangwyn share a somewhat negative attitude towards conventional religion and the Roman Catholic church in particular. Brangwyn swiftly withdraws his half-sister from a convent school when she becomes his ward, and Jelkes has abandoned a vocation for the priesthood after having been a Jesuit novice. The first enables Dion Fortune to express some of her reservations about the constricting effect of Christian attitudes to sexual morality, in which, in her day, she was by no means alone. The second gives her the chance to draw attention to the powerful effect of visualisation exercises, such as the *Spiritual Exercises of St Ignatius of Loyola*, the founder of the Jesuits, which are used as a means of training in that powerful order.

She also uses the situation of Jelkes' instruction of Hugh Paston to drop a few more pointers to recommended reading, rather more specifically than she did in *The Winged Bull*. Hugh has come upon a reference to a Black Mass in A.E.W. Mason's detective story *The Prisoner in the Opal* and also in the *fin de siécle* aesthetic decadence of the novels of Huysman, in *La Bas* and *A Rebours*. He points Hugh towards *The Devil's Mistress* by Brodie Innes and Naomi Mitcheson's *The Corn King and the Spring Queen*.

Brodie Innes was the head of the Alpha et Omega Temple offshoot of the Hermetic Order of the Golden Dawn into which Dion Fortune was initiated in 1919 and his novel *The Devil's Mistress* tells the story of sober Scottish housewives breaking out from a restrictive Calvinism with various churchyard antics deriving from medieval witchcraft. Their motivation has some relevance to Hugh Paston's situation, for he seeks to find a way to break out from his own constricting life – albeit that of a fashionable socialite. He seeks a more positive way however than what he has read so far. To his mind the Black Mass and medieval witchcraft were, each in their way, unbalanced means of rebelling against a suffocating religious ambience in their respective societies, Catholic or Calvinist, and he wonders if the ancient Dionysian mysteries, as portrayed in *The Bacchae* by Euripedes, might have played a similar function in ancient Greece.

A more constructive way of bringing through elemental power in ancient times is described in Naomi Mitcheson's *The Corn King and the Spring Queen*, although as Hugh observes, lying with a priestess on a platform over a ploughed field seems not to be entirely practicable nowadays. But he is highly interested in what Iamblichos has to say in *The Egyptian Mysteries* about the invisible powers being induced to manifest through the god forms by being built up in the imagination of the celebrants.

It is from a conflation of all this reading that he formulates the idea of fitting up a place as a temple where he can build up an imaginative contact with the pagan gods. In a highly pragmatic way he suggests that there must be some middle ground between the Catholic Mass and the Black Mass – and more than one sort of contact with the vast expanse of the Unseen between extremes of the divine and the diabolic.

Such practical conclusions have never entered Jelkes' head whose metaphysical quest since his retreat from the seminary has been more that of the mystical contemplative than the practical occultist. Dion Fortune traces his progress through the metaphysical philosophers Novalis, Hegel and Hinton and from thence to Madame Blavatsky, in whose writings he finds useful pointers, even if as Maurice Maeterlink has remarked, they might resemble the disorganised clutter of a builder's yard. Jelkes has also studied Freud and found him rather hard going unless interpreted through the Greek Dionysiac philosophy, where Priapus and Silenus are gods, not dirty little boys, and also where the full Olympean pantheon can be taken into account, including the likes of golden Aphrodite and Apollo. In fact he regards Freud, along with the materialist philosopher

Herbert Spencer as symptoms of decomposing Christianity, and he feels he has found superior wisdom in Petronius.

He is now faced with Hugh Paston determined to do something more practical than read books about the unseen worlds, and bent on getting in touch with the old forgotten forces hinted at by Iamblichos, Mitcheson, Innes and the like. To Jelkes' mind they are subjective rather than objective forces but even so realises that the personal hells or heavens that might be opened by such means could seem no less real to the rash invoker. He comforts himself by viewing Hugh's project somewhat in the light of a psychoanalytic process, much as Colonel Brangwyn in *The Winged Bull* introduced occultism to Ted Murchison in terms of a psychological experiment.

His approach uses a somewhat truncated version of events in Celtic legend when King Arthur, before being regarded as a Christian king and ideal of chivalry, set off to harry Hell because the Devil had overstepped his limits. And how he came away with the Devil's cooking pot which he gave to the earth goddess Keridwen, who minded it over a perpetual fire on the flanks of Snowdon as an inexhaustible source of food and drink. And how after Arthur became a perfect Christian monarch Keridwen's pot became the Holy Graal.

Paston however is more attracted to ancient Greek tradition. He is also intelligent enough to know that he is not going to evoke some kind of cosmic goat to materialise before him. Rather, he feels that something within his aura (the opal of Mason's book *The Prisoner in the Opal*) has gone septic, and that he needs to be able to break through into a wider inner world that corresponds to it, in order to find healing. Whilst this may not be what is generally called "spiritual" in the religious sense of the word, it is seems to him to be something good and vital with which he needs to make contact.

When he is thinking through this the following night Hugh comes in effect to a discovery of the aims and practicalities of magic, gleaned from his perusal of Jelkes' bookshelves. This has included, incidentally, what Dion Fortune coyly refers to as "four tattered, dog-eared, paper-backed volumes on magic spelt with a K". This is clearly an oblique reference to *Magick* by Aleister Crowley, for whom she had a certain regard despite his dubious reputation.

Hugh thinks the principle of a magician surrounding himself with symbols of a particular potency in order to concentrate the focus of consciousness is no different from a religious Easter retreat by his High Church friends. And he sees the physical furnishing of a temple as simply an extension of the principles of the visualisation exercises of Ignatius of Loyala's *Spiritual Exercises*. Whilst there are some who might regard this as blasphemous he argues that he has no intention of deliberately desecrating holy things. Certainly this is the kind of thing that one of Huysman's characters indulged in, but such an act would only have meaning for someone who believed in it, who had been, and who still was in an inverted sense, a practising Catholic.

He concludes therefore that a Black Mass is on a par with writing rude words on a lavatory wall. It is a pathetic, negative kind of thing, that is at best a destructive way of freeing oneself of inhibitions, and much the same could be said for Brodie Innes' *Isabel Goudie* and her churchyard antics. Thoughts of working a ritual on the naked flesh of a virgin have no great fascination for someone like Hugh, familiar with West End cabaret where naked flesh is put on view far more provocatively.

The suggestion that the flying ointment of the witches was simply an aphrodisiac with which they drugged themselves to provoke illusions of flying, Hugh sees as simply another form of the temple sleep that was induced in ancient Greek temples of healing. And whilst there may be a certain naivety about some of his conclusions, nonetheless the more he thinks about it all, the more he comes to conclude that all these methods, whatever their specific aims, are very much the same.

As a start he tries deliberately to invoke a dream for himself by lying on his back as he prepares for sleep and building in his mind a scene from ancient Greece. He imagines the sparse woods of oak and fir, the sea beyond, the sound of the bees and sight of the lizards basking in the sun, and flocks of mountain goats springing from rock to rock. He imagines he hears the sound of a goat-herd's pipes, which at any moment might perhaps turn into the pipes of Pan himself. He smells the pines on the dry air, feels the sun upon his skin, and hears the sound of the sea on the rocks beneath and then the crying of sea birds. This pulls him up with a start for he is not sure whether he has heard them in imagination or not – they seem to have appeared of their own accord.

This mental questioning breaks the magic and he is aware of himself in bed again, the images he has been building far away from normal consciousness. Nonetheless he feels that something of what he has experienced has been real, it has a vivid kind of quality about it.

Such visionary experience can very well trigger subsequent significant imagery. Thus as Hugh settles for sleep, he lets his mind wander over various memories that rise spontaneously into his mind. This includes running a race at school in sunshine much like that which he has just imagined in ancient Greece. Then of looking at his wife's naked back as she sits before a dressing table mirror, until he receives a shock when she turns to speak to him and for a brief flash reveals the face of a stranger.

Drifting in that somnambulistic realm of consciousness between waking and sleeping, he finds himself running on the Greek hillside, pursuing that same naked back that runs before him in the form of a Greek girl. However he cannot overtake her and in the end finds himself lost, deep in a wood amongst the dense growth of dark laurels and feels the touch of a sudden curious fear, almost a flash of panic. This, did he but know it, is an objective contact with the unseen world. The surge of panic is a reaction associated with the god Pan – from whose name the word derives.

He sits up in bed, startled and now fully awake, staring into the darkness. He sees or hears nothing, but to his nose there comes an unmistakable smell of burning. He leaps out, thinking the place to be on fire, and rouses Jelkes, but nothing is to be found, save, when they return to his room, the traces of that slight distinct smell together with faint blue wreaths of smoke in the candlelight.

We are left in some doubt as to whether or not this is a physically objective event or not. And it has to be said that after some intense interior visual experiences minor phenomena of this nature are not unknown, hovering between the boundaries of the objective and subjective, for the olfactory sense is closely akin to the psychic senses as is the sight of some evanescent form such as mist or smoke. From the way that Paston occasionally picks up telepathically on Jelkes' thoughts, it would appear that he is some way to being naturally psychic. However, even Jelkes is aware of the burning smell, which he identifies as cedar wood, and volunteers the opinion that its origin is not of this plane of existence. Paston of course is overjoyed at this, but Jelkes considerably less so.

In this sequence Dion Fortune has been describing the magical technique of the "composition of place", alternatively called the "composition of mood", for the attunement of mood should be the effect of a visualisation of a specific type of location. In latter years it has become more widely known as "path working" after its practice in relation to symbolic Paths of the Qabalistic Tree of Life. Psychologists such as Assegioli have called it "initiated symbol projection", whilst the Golden Dawn papers referred to it somewhat grandiloquently as "scrying in the spirit vision". Whatever the name, the technique is much the same.

Dion Fortune was an early enthusiast of the theory of ley-lines and esoteric power centres, and takes the opportunity to invest Mona Wilton with a practical knowledge of these things. So when Hugh begins his hunt for a suitable location for his magical experiments she helps him study a map to find suitable lines of power.

We have met these ideas before in *The Winged Bull*, but here we are given rather more detail. Mona points out how the stone circles of Avebury are the centre for the old sun worship, and so a suitable place for their work might well be on a line from there to some other powerful site. She advises against the actual major sites where the old gods have been worshipped, as the number of tourists will hamper sufficient seclusion for serious esoteric work – even in those days before tourism had become a major industry.

Getting to work with a ruler they locate another centre to the west, Tintagel in Cornwall, the reputed birth place of King Arthur, and draw a line across country to the east, through Avebury, which leads towards St. Albans, place of martyrdom of the first British saint. Similarly a roughly north-south line is drawn from St Alban's Head (alternatively St Alden's Head) in Dorset through Avebury, up to Lindisfarne, a major northern power centre. It may be remembered that in *The Winged Bull* this line was considered a great divide between Celtic and Viking traditions.

Mona also recommends finding a place that stands upon chalk, on the grounds that the earliest civilisations in the British Isles were upon the chalk downs, and also to look for sites of standing stones and hammer pools in the more detailed tracing of ley lines. She goes on to explain to the enthusiastically pagan Hugh Paston that the earlier saints are but early Christian overlays for the old gods, just as many cathedrals are built upon old pagan sites. That is another reason why those who would seek to worship the old gods should choose sites along a line between power centres rather than at the centres themselves, which may well have become fully Christianised over the centuries. Many such sites are dedicated to St. Michael the archangel whose traditional function is to put down the forces of the underworld, for Christians thought the old gods to be synonymous with the Devil, and she cites the St. Michael's church tower at the top of Glastonbury Tor, St. Michael's Mount in Cornwall and Mont St. Michel in Brittany, three sites, she claims, that make up a perfect triangle.

Paston, reverting somewhat to Jelkes' psychological point of view, opines that, in an enlightened age, the old gods are simply the same thing as the Freudian subconscious. Mona, however, hints that there may well be more to them than that!

This point tends to be borne out by the remainder of the book, for did he but know it Hugh's visionary experience has made sufficient contact with the unseen to set a train of events in motion. He has effectively awoken the forces of Pan in the first steps of an initiation process that will lead, through a series of subjective realisations, to certain objective circumstances and events.

The first of these events is that the site that they light upon has been an old monastic institution that has been subverted to pagan rites in medieval times, whilst its more ancient antecedents are suggested by the name of the local village, Thorley "Thor's Ley" and its significantly named public hostelry "The Green Man". (This derivation has previously been used, incidentally, by Dr Taverner in relation to Thursley, near his nursing home, but similar instances are commonplace throughout the British Isles.)

Having selected this place, Monk's Farm, as a site for his magical experiment, Hugh becomes more and more intrigued with the story of Ambrosius, the monk allegedly walled up as punishment for pursuing the worship of strange gods. What is more, it appears that there may well be more to Hugh's obsession with Ambrosius than a psychological identification, which becomes more vivid after Mona introduces him to the idea of reincarnation. He then begins to wonder if he had not been Ambrosius in a former life.

There is a certain amount of support for this theory when an illuminated manuscript is found containing a miniature portrait of Ambrosius. The face and figure, at any rate to Mona's mind, bear a remarkable resemblance to Hugh. Whilst Hugh himself has a dream in which he finds himself as Ambrosius, walled up and dying, until he escapes into a sunny Greek landscape with a female companion.

Both these elements could of course well be the result of self suggestion on the part of Hugh or Mona but even Jelkes is somewhat disposed to go along with the idea because of the combination of various circumstances. And from his acquaintance with esoteric theory he comes forth with the idea that when someone has been on the initiatory path, circumstances may well conspire to bring them back to it again, even taking them to the place of their last death – perhaps on the premise that death and initiation are a similar process, initiation leading to a second birth.

Hugh, increasingly fascinated with the story of Ambrosius, spends some time imagining the state of mind that might have led the medieval monk to a practical pursuit of ancient pagan rites. Part of the legend of the monk is that his ghost had returned to bring comfort to those of his companions who survived him when they were confined to penal conditions for the rest of their own lives. From this Hugh begins to theorise that if such ghostly visitations were true then it should be possible to invoke this ghostly presence now, perhaps calling in the services of a spiritualist medium. Jelkes, needless to say, strongly deprecates all thought of this.

However, further pursuit of that line becomes redundant as Hugh begins to feel the presence of Ambrosius himself, not as a ghostly figure objectively seen, but as a presence that seems to be at one with his own consciousness. It manifests as a kind of temporary overshadowing or obsession, and becomes sufficiently strong to alter his physical appearance to some extent, the features of the ancient monk building up over his own. This is a phenomenon not uncommon in certain types of spiritualist séance.

This presence, be it overshadowing ghost or secondary personality, appears to take over Hugh so dramatically that one confrontation with it shocks Mona into a nervous crisis with a physical repercussion that affects her health. The incident also goes some way to persuade Hugh's relations that they are witnessing the first signs of insanity. With an eye to their share of the family fortune, (a favourite theme with Dion Fortune in some of the Taverner stories) they take steps to have him certified. This is thwarted however, largely by the efforts of Jelkes, who knows full well the psychological dangers faced by Hugh but considers there to be better ways of dealing with them than confining him in a psychratric hospital.

A point that has sometimes been made in the theory of trance states and psychic experience is that they can be magnified if there is sympathetic involvement by other parties present. This seems to be borne out by spiritualist experience where a sympathetic and believing audience can improve phenomena whereas a cynical or sceptical audience can go some way to inhibit it. If this is the case, then Mona's and Jelkes' acceptance of Hugh's belief in the reality and presence of Ambrosius will have gone some way to increase this sense of presence. Hugh also discovers for himself a technique whereby he can make greater contact with the consciousness of the medieval monk, not by concentrating upon an image of him, but by consciously and deliberately identifying with him.

This is an interesting observation in light of Dion Fortune's trance experience and technique. One method that she used was to concentrate upon the image of the face of one of her inner contacts in preparing for verbal communication.

What Hugh is discovering for himself are some of the techniques of autosuggestion as well as those of spiritualism and magic. It is the kind of thing which, if uncontrolled, can be a slippery slope that can lead, in an unstable character, to an involuntary manifestion of multiple personalities and even schizophrenia, which is one reason for the insistence on careful and graded training in any bona fide esoteric school.

In Hugh Paston's case this becomes a dilemma for all of them. How do they tell the difference between a dissociated personality and a spirit control, or either from the powerful memory of a previous incarnation?

This butts upon a theory in Dion Fortune's researches into esoteric medicine, the so-called "doctrine of the ghost" whereby if a fragment of experience from a previous incarnation is not absorbed into higher consciousness in the after death condition, it may manifest as a psychological complex in a subsequent life. It may then perhaps be resolved, but if deliberately avoided for life after life becomes an aspect of karma. However this was part of her less publicised work, at first undertaken with her husband Dr. Penry Evans, and not publicly revealed until some years later, and then only in part or on restricted circulation, and eventually published as *Principles of Esoteric Healing*[1].

Following these subjective realisations Hugh discovers traces of an ancient chapel that would seem to have been used for Ambrosius' heretical rites. It contains the remains of a Tree of Life emblazoned upon one wall, whilst the circle of the zodiac is to be found surrounding a central point representing the Four Elements of the Earth, about which are engraved depictions of the seven planets.

However this is but the overlay of a more ancient stratum of practice and belief concerning the great god Pan whose presence is beginning to make itself increasingly felt, not least in the increased sexual proclivities of the two servants they hire, who in the novel also serve as a light comic relief, a favoured device of Dion Fortune in some of her minor characters. That the presence of Pan has also been an underlying one before being restimulated by Hugh seems evident from the tradition

---

[1] *Principles of Esoteric Healing*, Thoth Publications, 2006.

that the old buildings of Monks Farm have been a favoured trysting place for courting couples.

The approach to a formalised Rite of Pan is somewhat tentative and experimental, but it centres around the remains of this discovered temple and there is an interesting resonance with one of the images of the Tarot. When Hugh and Mona stand hand in hand in the darkness of this old temple, like a couple about to be married, they are described as facing an altar that is no longer there, but which if it had been "would have been the throne of the goat-god".

This image is reminiscent of the Tarot image of the Devil with its hideous distorted goat form, for which Aleister Crowley, in his Tarot published a few years later, substituted the figure of Pan. It is interesting to speculate if there had been any discussion or interchange between the two along these lines, or even if Crowley had picked up the idea from the novel. The association of goat-god and devil raises a whole raft of considerations about the Christian idea of evil and its association with the ancient gods. This was a matter close to the heart of Dion Fortune, who like many of her contemporaries felt there to be an altogether unhealthy sense of repression in church attitudes to sexual morality. To her mind, the Christian sexual ethic had been distorted by St. Augustine, whom she considered to be a debaucher with a mother fixation ruthlessly exploited by his mother, St. Monica, in order to convert him. She was similarly scathing about some of the less reported practices of the associates of St Francis, nor did cases of child abuse in the ecclesiastical domain escape her vitriolic attention.

She also casts her net wide in citing the strange case of the Knights Templar, who despite their rigorous moral code were accused by church and state authorities of worshipping a devilish figure known as Baphomet. In her view, similar ignorant or deliberate misunderstanding was accorded the pagan Mysteries by the early Christians, and in particular she has in mind a possible climax of the Eleusinian Mysteries when high priest and chief priestess descend into the darkness of the crypt to consummate a union that is a sacrament in intention and effect.

Mona goes forward with Hugh's intentions on the strength of a feeling of dedication to all that is natural and true and good. In a rather striking image she sees Pan as a leader of the goats as opposed to the church which she feels is a leader of the sheep. She imagines Pan as a kind of underworld Apollo, holding out a crook to lead the creatures of the flock of Ishmael, the misfits who find no place in the world of towns and men – the keeper of all wild and hunted souls. Thus the real invocation of Pan is a surrender to the bed rock of natural fact rather than a striving after an unreal spirituality. Whereas St Francis spoke contemptuously of the body as Brother Ass she sees man as a centaur, akin to the winged horse, Pegasus – and here we have a resonance with the imagery of *The Winged Bull*. Mona feels reassured, come what may, and feels that she has the blessing of Pan. This combination of Biblical and pagan imagery is typical of Dion Fortune, and her sympathy with the latter is one facet of her having become something of an icon for the modern neo-pagan movement despite her, albeit unorthodox, Christian affiliations.

Mona feels an atmosphere of doom and impending evil and danger within the air on entering the underground temple where Hugh has been conducting the experiment of lying alone in the dark, dressed in monkish robes, identifying himself with Ambrosius. Breaking in upon him in this way is indeed not without danger, for her physical presence synchronises with the dreams of the walled up monk as conceived by Hugh, who is fantasising that at any moment the succuba of his dreams will open up his prison doors, and together they will enter into the green hills of ancient Greece.

With remarkable sensitivity Mona picks up intuitively upon this, and enters into a spontaneous ritual with him, taking on the role of the dream woman and leading him up the stairs toward the light. Here Hugh, still in a state of somnambulistic trance, turns aside into the passage where once the other monks had been imprisoned, and goes from door to door calling each by name. Mona is sufficiently into belief in the reality of this to wonder how many of such souls, reincarnated into the modern world, might at this point feel some vague stir of memory, some impulse from the unseen, in response to Hugh/Ambrosius' inner call.

Finally they stand face to face for some moments, part way in consciousness between present and past, as in the grip of this magical fantasy he enfolds her into his arms. Mona is aware of the possible danger in which she may be in this lonely place at the mercy of an unbalanced man, who could quite easily tip over the balance of reason into rape or even murder. However, fortunately nothing untoward takes place as Hugh integrates the projected element of his unfulfilled desires into himself, as they pull themselves back into normal consciousness.

Hugh is now able to muster a more objective view of the situation and tells her to return to the house, reverting half-jokingly to psychoanalytic mode in saying that he needs to be alone "to abreact his complexes". Mona withdraws, not entirely convinced by Hugh's glib assurances that in the full flow of any resulting catharsis all will be well. She feels there is likely to be more strain upon the integrity of his personality than he bargains for, that personalities can disintegrate under such strains, and that there are things, according to Jelkes, that happen in psychoanalysis that never get into the textbooks.

In this we have another glimpse of Dion Fortune in the role of psychotherapist. She had been an early student of psychoanalysis and at the time of writing these novels was in active correspondence with the Jungian Eranos Foundation in Zurich. Bernard Bromage, a London University academic who met her at about this time, has gone on record as saying that she seemed to have all the qualities to be a successful healer in her own right, and seemed able to quieten agitation and to still fears in others by her very presence. That she had a kind of maternal strength of receptiveness which led the most timid to confide in her, and he refers to some severe cases of collapse or serious obsession that she, working in collaboration with her husband, Dr Penry Evans, had handled and cured. All of which goes to show that she was well aware of the deeper side of occultism as opposed to its more usual superficial exploitation, and that she had gone some way to make of *The Secrets of Dr. Taverner* something of an achieved reality.

Hugh has spent his couple of hours in the dark cellar following through a mental discipline he has learned from Jelkes, of tracing things back from present events to past causes. This has led him back to thinking of Ambrosius with great intensity, reconstructing the medieval scene in which he had lived, experiencing his emotions and feeling his sensations. The result has been a kind of integration, almost as if the life of Ambrosius were a memory of an earlier part of his present life. Furthermore he has realised that the traumatic experiences of Ambrosius, if indeed they were part of a former life of his own, have resulted in a neurosis that is crippling his present personality. He reflects how Ambrosius had been a misfit in the cloister, being a natural child of nature in an ascetic culture, and that his own problem is much the same as that faced by Ambrosius. Ambrosius had found it catastrophic when he broke with monastic discipline to seek the natural things that were denied him, and now Hugh finds he suffers from the same inhibitions, although they are now part and parcel of his own soul.

He is mortally afraid of coming to grips with natural things – suffering from an inherent belief that the primitive and the catastrophic are inalienably linked. As a consequence his whole life has been lived at a superficial level. He cannot come to terms with the problems that had caused such suffering to Ambrosius.

Ambrosius was no devotee of the devil but one who was born out of due season, who found himself in the wrong place at the wrong time. Hugh wonders if he can go back beyond Ambrosius and his dreadful tragedy, and make contact with what had gone before in a previous life, that is epitomised by the vision of ancient Greece and joy in the primitive nature forces.

He now comes to the startling realisation that his original plan to evoke Pan has been the start of a process that is still going on. He has evoked a particular "presence" by his imaginative composition of place. When he invoked Pan in Jelkes' old establishment, he contacted a presence that had caused circumstances to bring him to the appropriate place with the opportunity to continue further.

The philosophy of all this does not concern him too much. Like Dion Fortune and many other practical occultists his approach is entirely pragmatic. For what is reality and what is fantasy in all of this? Is Hugh Paston more real than Ambrosius? Are either of them more real than the scenes from ancient Greece? If any of these is taken to be the one reality, then the others might be relegated to fantasy. Yet taken together they are as the hands of a clock corresponding to a passage of time, markers on the face of a dial that is the ever changing experience of the immortal human soul as it uses different personalities as masks.

Jelkes may strive to talk learnedly on the metaphysics of all his, but it is Mona who gets results by believing in the different elements at face value, simply taking them for granted. For her, Ambrosius is as real as Hugh Paston, as are the boy and girl in ancient Greece. That is to say, the power of magic comes from faith and belief, however naïve and simplistic this may seem.

Hugh now has a feeling that he has made a great breakthrough in having at last, in his recent enfolding of Mona in his arms, enabled Ambrosius to embrace his succuba. Moreover, it was a spontaneous act from the depths of his soul, breaking through the social conventions ingrained in his present personality. He feels now that the unquiet monk will walk no more. Whatever terminology might be used, psychological or esoteric, a great change has been effected, nothing will be quite the same again.

Dion Fortune has packed a considerable body of magical theory and practice into all of this. Ambrosius had begun as an idea in Hugh's mind that has gradually taken hold of his imagination to the point where it has passed into the vividness of a dream, and upon which has been built a surrounding framework of day dream into which the figure of Ambrosius has been projected with almost lunatic intensity. Where is the line to be drawn in all this? What is the relationship between the day dream and the reality? Has one brought about the other?

In discussing this with Jelkes, the old bookseller asks him why he is so sure that Ambrosius and he are one. To which Hugh can only reply because he has a kind of inner conviction about it. That Ambrosius represents something in his makeup that goes very deep, so that whether he be fact or fancy he is worth cultivating. This had occurred more powerfully after Mona had come along and started talking about reincarnation. As a result of this he had begun readily to identify with Ambrosius, and the more he did so the more impressed people became. One practical result of this was that he developed a more positive and outgoing personality, standing up to members of his family who had for so long taken him for granted. Jelkes agrees that at least he has gained increased self-confidence and so, if nothing else, identification with Ambrosius has been a very effectual method of induced auto-suggestion.

However, in his heart of hearts Hugh feels there must be something more to it than that, and that Ambrosius pertains to a level of reality that he cannot describe. He cares little whether Ambrosius be called dissociated complex, past incarnation, or just plain delusion. It is belief in him that works. There seems to him little help in a purely psychological approach. He feels that the practical way forward must be to continue with the invocation of Pan, which has brought up the figure of Ambrosius and his problems as a first stage, which he has now faced and resolved. From now on the question is how best to evoke Pan, not in ancient or medieval terms but in a fashion appropriate to the present day.

Jelkes agrees that it therefore seems best to continue to take Ambrosius at face value, just as one takes a bank note at face value when spending it. It also apparent to him that Hugh has been working with power all along, whether or not he has realised it, and whether the power be labelled objective or subjective makes little difference.

To Jelkes, Pan acts very much as a general opener to the subconscious, to the racial memory, to the biological memory, or the morphological memory – simply because he stands for lack of repression. From this the way can eventually lead to any of the more specialised gods and elevated gods of Mount Olympus. In a final summing up of where they are at, he recommends reading Jung's *The Secret of the Golden Flower*, together with Coué on induced autosuggestion, Iamblichos on the bringing of power to the Egyptian gods by the force of imagination, and St Ignatius on the visualisation training of the Jesuits.

Nonetheless the practical work that Jelkes has in mind for Hugh partakes more of psychology than occultism, although in the event it develops into a halfway house that leads from one to the other His aim is to take Hugh into the chapel to build up the Ambrosius fantasy and then psychoanalyse it. To assist his identification Hugh dresses up in monk's robes, and Mona, almost on a whim, casts off her usual dowdy clothes to appear in a long green dress and golden sandals, a fillet in her hair, rather in the fashion of an ancient priestess. It is thus in its beginnings a somewhat dramatic form of psychoanalyis, complete with altar, candles and incense, with Mona sat opposite to Hugh with the idea of picking up the transference from Hugh when it occurs.

All begins in somewhat pedestrian fashion as Jelkes and Hugh more or less intellectualise their theories until the point Mona spontaneously intervenes with an account of daydreams that she has had since she was a child. It appears that they accord closely with Hugh's fantasies of ancient Greece. This mutual meeting in fantasy having been established she more or less takes control and leads the two men out of the chapel into the moonlit meadow outside. Here she commences what she calls her moon dance.

From Jelkes' description this would appear to have consisted outwardly of suggestive and sensuous movements of sexual provocation but chastely performed at some distance from Hugh. As such they might well have been hardly more than what he might have seen more expertly done in West End cabaret. However, in this case we have another dimension added, of polar exchange of animal magnetism from aura to aura. We have had a similar view of this kind of working between Ursula and Ted in *The Winged Bull*, only in that situation Ursula had been projecting magnetism to the depleted Ted. In this instance Mona appears to be drawing magnetism out of the desperately repressed Hugh.

In a heightened state of psychic awareness such as can be induced on such occasions, Jelkes is aware of lines of force emanating from her hands towards Hugh, who is induced into a sort of etheric projection, at which point a simulacrum of Ambrosius stands out before him, separate from Hugh's physical body.

This has now gone far beyond any theories of psychoanalysis, for Jelkes, even with his limited psychism, is aware of forces that have been evoked between them, perhaps restimulating what the monk Ambrosius had evoked in his ancient rites. Strong powerful elemental forces and forms seem to be surrounding and pressing in on them whilst in the centre can be seen the ghostly figure of Ambrosius with the female succuba form that he had created by his own desires and his subtle arts in medieval times.

Then slowly this vision and its atmosphere fades, and they return more or less to normal consciousness but aware that they have experienced something profoundly moving, out of this world and difficult to understand. They spend the rest of the evening trying to come to terms with what they have evoked, released or exorcised, conscious that this is beyond the catharsis of a psychoanalysis and is some kind of balancing up of ancient magical forces.

The next day too is largely taken up with psychological introspection as to what all this means but it is Hugh who makes the greatest progress, coming to a realisation of what magic, in its deeper sense (which is that of the ancient Mysteries) is all about. In a series of questions about current religious attitudes, he comes to one that carries within itself an answer that was no doubt close to Dion Fortune's mind. Are the descending Holy Spirit and the uprising Pan two opposing forces locked in eternal struggle - or are they an alternating current playing between two poles of spirit and matter?

Metaphysics aside, he knows what his immediate needs are, and these revolve around Mona. But there is more to it than the simple image of a boy and girl on the sunny hills of ancient Greece. They are mature modern people who seek more from a mating than the simple animal pleasures of the young Greeks. In Mona's fantasy she has moved on to see herself as a priestess initiated into the Mysteries by a male priest.

This stimulates a further fantasy of his own of being a high priest in the sanctuary in the Eleusinian Mysteries, awaiting the coming of the priestess, who, as she appears through the curtain from the outer world, is revealed to be Mona in the robe of a priestess of Ceres. Behind him is the All-Father, behind her the Earth-Mother. In the fantasy he realises that the priest has now become a god as the divine power flows through him, so that he becomes part of a greater whole, at one with the earth as it swings through the heavens.

Suddenly though he is pulled up short, as he comes back to his present personality and realises that there is no priestess before him in reality. And at the thought of the real life Mona he realises that to attract her he needs to be more like the powerful and courageous Ambrosius than himself. In his unreconstructed state he had hardly been very attractive to Mona, or indeed perhaps to any woman save a motherly or caring type. But even so, the power generated in Ambrosius had been born not out of realisation but out of frustration, and there is no mileage in trying to dramatize a frustration. It then occurs to him that he will never again turn into Ambrosius for the simple reason that Ambrosius has turned into him. In other words he has laid the ghost by aiming to fulfil the things which frustrated him.

His mind goes back to the time when, goaded by his sister's innuendoes, he had fantasised the death of Ambrosius in the chapel. With this had come the strange certainty of a promise of achievement in the end. But what was it that had been promised to Ambrosius? What had he sought? Might not that promise to a former incarnation be fulfilled in his present personality in this incarnation? Turning his mind back to Arcady he sees the god Pan with his shepherd's pipe as the source of inspiration that he must go after, and that there is no diabolical deity like the Goat of Mendes as the perverted imagination of the medieval world has tried to make of it. He reflects on the great civilising benefits of the Renaissance, when Europe awoke from its medieval dream to recover the great gifts of the ancient world. Those gifts that had been condemned and rejected by the advance of the early church. Was there about to be a new awakening in our own day? A much wider one – heralded by the psychoanalysis of Freud. A modern version of "Great Pan is risen!". And he goes on to wonder how far the realisation of an idea by one person might inject an idea into the group mind of the race, like yeast working a ferment, for his own problems seem but a reflection of the age at large.

The purpose of the fertility rite in the ploughing field in *The Corn King and the Spring Queen* had been to link up the forces behind the earth and that of the sun, all for the sake of the tribe. But had the couple who had undertaken the rite first linked up to those forces themselves? Bringing this through to modern times, was it possible for a couple, duly dedicated, to bring something through into the group mind of the race that added to and benefited the racial heritage? Simply to be something, and to do something that the group soul of the race would feel subconsciously. It was the way that Jelkes said that adepts worked.

It seems to him that this is something that he can pull off with Mona, on account of the similarity of their fantasies. It is no longer the private problem of a man in love with a woman who does not respond to him, but the question of restoring balance to an unbalance by letting himself by borne by the cosmic tides. It was the way to set invisible causes in motion – provided it lies along the line of their course.

These cosmic tides and invisible causes are of course the master in these situations. It is not a matter of personal preference.

All this is very much a justification for Dion Fortune's belief in the power and effectiveness of magic, and it very much needs this latter qualification. For if everyone had the power to go into subjective states in order to affect the subconscious mind of the race then goodness knows what mischief might not be wrought. This perhaps was one reason for the intense secrecy current in senior occult ranks at one time. However, things are not quite so easy as that. For nothing can be effected that is not in line with inner tides and inner realities, one can simply help the cosmic tides along, not arbitrarily redirect them. And it is a reflection of this that caused Dion Fortune in her training of initiates to lay so much emphasis upon the principle of service and dedication to higher principles.

Hugh Paston now feels that he has stumbled upon a very important key, by realising that the approach to dynamic reality lies in the path of fantasy, the most powerful form of auto suggestion - a point which orthodox psychologists have never realised.

How however could he ordain himself a priest of a forgotten rite? The only way seems to be to let the power rise within him of its own peculiar magnetism, so that deep calls to deep. Mona had done much the same thing in her moon dance and now it was his turn to reciprocate.

He turns to the practicalities of furnishing a temple to Pan appropriately, which he feels would certainly not be in the Victorian Gothic style which seems so popular with esoteric enthusiasts. Modern functional furniture seems to him more effective as a run through of force into form.

However, the most appropriate temple is soon revealed to him with the synchronicity of his finding an ancient site in the nearby woods, in the shape of a vesica piscis surrounded by ancient yew trees and with a fallen stone in the centre, which he restores to upright position – a fairly overt symbolic act in view of the fact that its shape is obviously phallic. He has also inadvertently brushed up against some herbs that Mona has planted that have the very strong aroma of the billy goat.

In a romantic novel written in the nineteen thirties for nineteen thirties readers it is obvious that Hugh and Mona must first render themselves respectable by conventional marriage, but this is matter of factly dealt with and leads naturally to the scenario of their wedding night. This is spent in the oval of yew trees facing each other across the standing stone as he raises one hand in ancient priestly salute to the invincible sun, and placing the other hand flat between Mona's breasts he utters the great cry of the climax of the ancient Mysteries, - "Be far from us, O ye profane, for the coming of the god is at hand!"

Part Three

The Mysteries of the Sea and Moon

Chapter Five
The Sea Priestess

The Story

Sea Priestess is told in the person of Wilfred Maxwell, an estate agent in a small west country town, with artistic ambitions and an urge to escape to London. However family circumstances prevent him from doing so, with moral obligations towards an invalid mother and an elder sister which the women exploit to the full. A family quarrel brings on the first of a number of asthma attacks in which, as a result of the medication he has been given, he enters into a psychic condition as he gazes at the moon through his sick room window.

He achieves a limited amount of independence from his female relations by setting up a bachelor flat in old outbuildings at the bottom of the garden, overlooking a small tidal stream, and also comes across some theosophical books which introduce him to the idea of reincarnation. He diverts himself by making up historical fantasies of what he might have been in previous lives, and these take on a particular vividness whenever he is in a comatose state between sleeping and waking. He supplements these experiences with reading the occultly atmospheric works of Algernon Blackwood and also comes across *The Projection of the Astral Body* by Muldoon and Carrington, which encourages him to make desultory but unsuccessful attempts at much the same thing.

His fascination for spinning stories and dreaming dreams of past incarnations meets with a depressing rebuff when he attends a local lecture on reincarnation and finds himself in the company of a number of enthusiasts whose ideas seem manifestly delusory. After this he concentrates more upon "feeling with" things, particularly with the moon, as he had done in his initial experience, and also with the sea, in communion with a tidal stream that flows beneath his window.

Then deeply drugged after a particularly bad asthmatic attack he finds himself in a vivid dream. He seems to be out on a nearby headland called Bell Head, although it looks somewhat different from its modern appearance. There is deep water instead of marshes inland from it, and what appear to be ancient coracles are pulled up on the strand. Then he sees a long low ship, propelled by banks of oars, coming in from the sea. It has a great purple sail emblazoned with a crimson dragon, and sitting in the high poop is a striking looking woman reading in a book. Somehow he knows it to be a high priestess who is expected to oversee the worship of the local people as a means of preventing further inundation of the land by the encroaching sea.

Soon after this experience he is called upon to meet an old client of his company, a Miss Vivien Le Fay Morgan, who has previously done business with his father. She is of remarkably youthful appearance despite what must be her considerable age, and to Wilfred Maxwell's eyes she bears a strong resemblance to the figure he saw in his dream.

It transpires that this lady has for some years been involved in psychic experiments with planchette and crystal ball, as a result of which she desires to find a suitable place in which to undertake some magical work. In his professional capacity Wilfred helps her in this search and discovers an old abandoned fort at the end of a rocky headland that projects into the sea. Encouraged by her interest in his artistic ambitions and psychic experiments, he undertakes the task of personally redecorating as well as overseeing restoration of the fort.

After she has moved in he becomes a frequent visitor, and in a vision that elaborates upon his initial dream, sees himself as a youth entrusted with lighting the flares to guide in her ship through the sea mists. He also feels that her visit is concerned with ancient worship related to the stone circles and caves facing the shoreline, traces of which still remain.

Their friendship grows with an exchange of psychic confidences but although it is plain that he is falling in love with her, she maintains a sympathetic but aloof stance, their relationship being largely confined to the pursuit of her magical aims and discussion of his psychic perceptions.

These take on increasing importance as they seek deeper visions in a "Fire of Azrael" made from selected woods, and she tells of ancient traditions revealed to her in her own psychic experiments, including a contact with a Priest of the Moon in whom she places great store, with teachings that hark back to the lost continent of Atlantis. Finally she reveals that she would like him to co-operate in her magical work and to act as priest to her priestess, in which role she will train him.

In further experiments with visions in the fire he sees himself entrapped in the nearby cave as a living sacrifice to the incoming sea. This is prelude to a severe attack of asthma that takes him close to death, in the course of which he has powerful visions of the sea gods, all with the physical synchronicity of a heavy storm.

As the time of the next full moon draws near Vivien Le Fay is strongly affected by the gathering power, going out to the end of the rocks to perform an invocation that seems to put her into an entranced state, whilst Wilfred, in the course of finishing his mural paintings, also experiences a strong contact with the Priest of the Moon.

She tells him to keep away from the fort until the next full moon while she prepares for the performance of an important ritual. This entails his waiting in a cave at the landward end of the down, and then to walk a sacred way marked out by her along the back of the down, to the fort. Here she performs with him a magical working with the powerful inner presence of the Priest of the Moon.

Wilfred then falls asleep and when he awakens next morning finds her gone. She has left as a farewell gift a necklace of star sapphires, together with a sealed note, to give to his wife whenever he should marry. The cave has also been mysteriously dynamited and the fort itself, after heavy storms, soon reverts to its uninhabitable state.

After the shock of her abrupt departure Wilfred finds that he has become a much more positive character, as his female relations and others soon discover. Despite their disapproval he courts and eventually marries Molly, a girl who works in his office, some ten years his junior and daughter of a local drunken bully.

Their marriage turns out however to be little more than humdrum until they begin to come to terms with the meaning of the gift of the star sapphires, and to act upon the advice of the note that comes with them, which is to meditate on the moon. This leads to a burgeoning magnetic relationship between Molly and Wilfred, and eventually to conscious contact with the Priest of the Moon as they develop a magical as well as marital partnership in their future life together.

*   *   *

This novel marks a change in Dion Fortune's fictional technique, as it written in the first person, ostensibly from the diaries of Wilfred Maxwell, as it tells the story of his meeting and working with the mysterious Miss Vivien Le Fay Morgan.

We also find her less concerned with the possible abuses of occultism. *The Secrets of Dr Taverner* and *The Demon Lover*, were quite lurid in this respect whilst *The Winged Bull* had its share in the doings of the malodorous Hugo Astley. In *The Goat-foot*

God and *The Sea Priestess*, as indeed in *Moon Magic* to follow, there are no out and out villains.

In one respect this may be an effort to depict the occult scene more as it is in real life rather than as a genre of adventure fiction. There is no doubt she enjoyed writing such stories and despite her heavy esoteric writing commitments she had begun to write some non-occult thrillers under the pen name of V.M. Steele where she could let herself go in terms of criminal skulduggery. These three books *The Scarred Wrists*, *Hunters of Humans* and *Beloved of Ishmael*, are virtually unobtainable nowadays, and like most popular fiction of the period are likely to remain so. They contain no esoteric interest and the closest they resemble the occult novels is a penchant for a heroine who brings about the redemption of a somewhat flawed male - although without the use of any magical skills.

It seems that her occult fictional work had less commercial success than its publishers desired, and that Williams and Norgate (who continued successfully to publish *The Mystical Qabalah*) decided to call a halt after the second novel, although the uncompromisingly magical sections of *The Sea Priestess* and its unconventional denouement may also have turned their faces against it. Nonetheless Dion Fortune had enough faith in the work to publish it herself and it is regarded by many readers to be her best.

Apart from the magical detail the respect accorded to *The Sea Priestess* is in no small part due to the powerful personality of its protagonist, the sea priestess herself. In a number of respects she is considerably larger than life and tends to provoke a strong reaction in readers, both positive and negative.

Those who only see her from the negative side see her as a heartless and manipulative vamp, an inveterate poseur who would only have fooled someone as innocent and vulnerable as the hen-pecked Wilfred Maxwell. However whilst he may well have exchanged one form of female domination for another, it must be said that at least at Miss Le Fay Morgan's hands he has a more enjoyable time of it. What is more, he comes out of their association as a far more positive and balanced character, able to put his life in better order than it was before the sea priestess arrived on the scene.

Any negative reaction in any of her readers would have come as no surprise to Dion Fortune, who in an article in her *Inner Light Magazine* claimed that in her novels she was aiming to perform a certain degree of psychoanalysis upon her readers, or even to give them the experience of an initiation if they cared to identify strongly with any of the characters. A strong negative reaction could well be part and parcel of this, and she cites with some amusement having received a returned copy of *The Winged Bull* with the comment from an outraged reader that it was too depraved even to throw into the dustbin for fear of corrupting the scavengers.

As an adept Vivien Le Fay Morgan is certainly a more colourful and overtly powerful character than Colonel Brangwyn, although she shares his aesthetic tastes, and she is certainly in a different league from Jelkes the bookseller and failed Jesuit. She seems to have been largely self taught in her magic, having come to her current position by way of the ouija board and the crystal ball. Nonetheless she has evidently used them to some effect, having over the years filled a number of notebooks with her records, and made contact with a powerful inner plane figure known as the Priest of the Moon.

Her meeting Wilfred, with his unique combination of artistic and professional skills and personal family circumstances help forward her plans. Much of Wilfred's talent for psychism comes fortuitously through narcotic medication, hardly to be recommended as a means of esoteric development, and although Vivien le Fay Morgan is happy to take advantage of that fact, she shows him more satisfactory means of developing his talents by means of meditation and ritual.

Wilfred also learns of the fine line to be drawn between different types of psychism. In the early days of his own self tuition he revels in fantasies of what might be memories of previous incarnations, but after attending the meeting where conflicting claims are made by gullible enthusiasts he learns to be somewhat suspicious of their validity. He feels he is treading on safer ground in feeling at one with the natural forces of the sea or moon. They bring with them a sense of fulfilment, and may well have subtly established the inner connections that lead to his meeting with Miss Le Fay Morgan.

Once the two have met, he feels, under her guidance, to be recovering valid memories that have connections with the locality. It is an evocative countryside both in fact and fiction. Bell Head exists in real life as Brean Down off the coast of Somerset. It is unique in facing directly onto the deep Atlantic, without the coasts of Wales or Ireland getting in the way, and forms part of a chalk ridge that makes up the local topography of hills, knolls and tors that once were islands in an archipelago of which Glastonbury Tor formed a part. Dion Fortune spent much of her schooldays near here and took the land into her consciousness to form the esoteric topography of the novel. Some of this is invented or adapted but much has a basis in fact.

Brean Down, now part of the National Trust, contains traces of civilisation and worship that go back through Romano-Celtic to Bronze Age and Neolithic times. The ruined fort at its end, dating from the 1860's was a defence against the French, was abandoned in 1900 after an accidental explosion at much the same time that Dion Fortune was a local schoolgirl, and this memory may have suggested the somewhat melodramatic dynamiting of the meditation cave in the novel.

Bell Knowle may well be the very prominent Brent Knoll just off the modern M5 motorway, whilst Dickmouth compares closely with the seaside resort of Weston-super-Mare. Dickford would seem to be the village of Axbridge, which sits on the River Axe, a river which Dion Fortune chose to call the Dick with a play on the name Naradek – which is traditionally the river which ran by the City of the Golden Gates in ancient Atlantis.

It is however upon the topography of the novel that we should concentrate and the psychic visions that Wilfred and Vivien weave about it. One lesson the novel teaches is the importance of fantasy, and whether such fantasy is objectively correct in all its details is to some extent a minor consideration, as long as it performs its fuction of carrying the main body of the work along. This applies not only to the surrounding countryside and the temple they build but also to Wilfred's vision of Vivien herself.

She later admits that her aloofness and power dressing form part of a deliberate technique to build up an aura of mystery about herself, but that if it began and ended there her construction of such an image would simply be a process of auto-suggestion that would remain entirely subjective.

However, if she can induce others to share that vision, and picture her as she pictures herself, then "things begin to happen". When their suggestion aids her autosuggestion, the combined imagery will take a quantum leap into a state of inner objectivity. In conventional esoteric terms, a form will have been built upon the astral ethers that can become the channel for occult forces.

The rationale behind the magic would however be of little moment without the ability to tap, as the main source of power, the inner tides of moon and the sea under the direction of the Priest of the Moon. And this is what distinguishes what would otherwise be no more than the superficial trappings of a poseur from the successful role playing and image making of an adept.

Something of the type of the forces that she has in mind are revealed when she goes out onto the sea swept rocks when the moon is approaching its full and chants an evocation to Isis. And here it is important to realise just who or what is intended in her vision of the goddess Isis. She is a power that is veiled on Earth by the luminous garment of nature, but can be imagined unveiled in the heavens in the radiance of the moon's reflected light. Thus she is appropriately evoked at the time of the full moon, although not specifically identified with the moon but with the entire divine feminine principle. This is evoked under a variety of names, associated with the heavens and with the earth itself and the sea.

Isis Veiled is Our Lady of Nature, Isis Unveiled is the Heavenly Isis, Ea is the soul of space and parent of time, Ge is the magnetic earth that forms an aura about the physical planet, Binah is the Great Sea of the Qabalah from whence all spiritual life arose, and beyond that the great Limitless Light of the Uncreate Realities from whence all creation springs. It is no petty sex magic that is being evoked here as a superficial reading of the text might seem to suggest.

Nor is it a mere theological abstraction as Wilfred realises when he looks into her eyes, and sees they are strange and wide and inhuman, not even the eyes of a priestess but of a goddess. At this point he has gone far beyond a mere personal infatuation, and when he returns to the fort to complete his wall painting, there remains but the face of the sea priestess to complete. Now under his brush he discovers he is painting not the face of the sea priestess, as he thought and intended, but that of the Priest of the Moon, the inner contact behind her work.

The figure is gazing into a crystal ball, which has been the mode through which Vivien contacted him in the past, and in this we are offered a glimpse of a reflective means of communication between the planes, each in their own plane of reality, using a similar device to contact the other, somewhat like a mobile video telephone.

Through Wilfred's picturing of him the Priest of the Moon begins to enter his life, and what at first seemed but a shadowy figure begins to take on the unseen presence of a dynamic personality. If this is but a product of his own subconscious then Wilfred feels that at least he has a subconscious of which he can be proud. Not infrequently he wonders whether he is deluding himself, or even losing his reason, but each time he feels the approach of the Priest of the Moon he feels the presence of a personality whose reality is beyond all doubting.

This leads him deeper into the field of ancient memories and into the legend of the lost continent of Atlantis. He sees a sacred city built upon the slopes of an extinct volcano with a wide alluvial plain stretching to a far line of mountains. In the centre of the city of white buildings is a great sun temple whose open court is of black and white paving and adorned with two great pillars that act as gnomons of a great time dial. It is a prototype of the Temple of Solomon. He sees the antecedents of the Priest of the Moon, as a keeper of the sacred flame in a deep underground temple, a volcanic flame of the deep earth itself.

One who was inspired to seek out the wisdom of an older faith when the priesthood of the Sun Temple began to face corruption, a faith that that worshipped the Great Mother through her forms of moon and sea. Eventually leading an expedition from the doomed continent he lands, via the Bermudas and the Azores, on the western coast of Ireland and from thence goes about the indigenous tribes of the islands of Britain, teaching his wisdom, in which lies the basis of what was later to be dimly remembered and recreated as the Arthurian Legend, and he himself to be recalled as Merlin.

The sea priestess on the other hand is also of Atlantean descent, member of a religious community founded on the western seaboard of Ireland from whence she has come to the mainland Atlantic coast in Wilfred's earlier visions. Here he further realises that he has in that ancient time been a sacrifice to the sea gods at the priestess's hands, although not before being allowed to possess her physically, in defiance of all priestly protocol. He compares these new realisations with

Morgan, who confirms that her own agree. And whether these are genuine memories of the remote past or a wish fulfilment fantasy with its roots in the present life is of no great matter, for either buttresses the other, to form a channel through which the higher forces can work.

The magical work builds up to its apogee after a meal where everything eaten has, by its shape or colour or associations, a symbolic connection to the moon - an interesting minor resonance with Aleister Crowley's occult novel *Moonchild*. Then Wilfred, clad in appropriately coloured robes, sits in meditation at the landward end of the Down in a cave that looks across to the remains of a cave in Bell Knowle where once he believes himself to have taken part in an altogether more serious ritual – sacrificing his life in the interests of the ancient tribe threatened with inundation from the sea. He then has to walk by moonlight along the lengthy processional way, between "moon pylons" rebuilt by Vivien, along to the fort where she awaits him to perform the rite towards which all this work has been building.

Whilst all this, if physically performed, would have been a somewhat unlikely scenario with many practical difficulties, visualised in the imagination it can be a powerful experience for the imaginative reader, which is very much what Dion Fortune had in mind when she wrote it.

Substantial parts of the rite are quoted in the novel, taken from Dion Fortune's *Rite of Isis* which she performed before invited audiences at the Belfry at much the same time she was writing the novel. The Belfry, a converted mid-19th century Presbyterian church that she had leased at this time, will appear again in her subsequent novel *Moon Magic*. She thus took this Isis work very seriously, and sought its expression by whatever means. She felt she was helping to inject into the group soul of the nation a healthier realisation of the forms of relationship possible between the sexes as well as the deep importance of the feminine principle.

The magical means whereby this might be effected would be by a man and woman identifying deliberately and closely with natural inner forces to form the circuit for a healing current between the spiritual and physical worlds. This, it may be recalled is much the same agenda pursued by Hugh Paston and Mona Freeman in *The Goat-foot God*, only whereas they stumbled upon it almost by accident the sea priestess is very well aware of what she is doing and how she means to do it.

As her friend Bernard Bromage has remarked, Dion Fortune favoured dressing in much the same style as the sea priestess at this time, with large floppy hats and high collars concealing the face, and a long dramatic dark cloak over a scarlet dress, together with chunky jewellery of which a necklace of star sapphires did form a part. A few years later however, when this phase of her work was over, he observes that she had adopted a more sober and quietly elegant form of dress.

Her approach to ritual technique at time of writing the novels seems to concentrate upon a one to one contra-sexual dynamic, under the aegis of a third over-seeing party. This is exemplified in the Brangwyn-Ursula-Ted triad in *The Winged Bull*, and, to a lesser extent, the Jelkes-Mona-Hugh scenario in *The Goat-foot God*. In both these fictional cases marriage is the end result, as was probably essential in popular fiction of the period, and the lack of such a straightforward denouement in *The Sea Priestess* may have caused the reluctance of her publishers to go ahead with it. There is no record that magical practice in her Fraternity at the time had as its aim either physical sex or marriage. As Vivien le Fay Morgan is at pains to point out in both *The Sea Priestess* and *Moon Magic* her aims completely transcend the physical level and the same may be said to apply to the real Dion Fortune.

An interesting change of dynamic in the sequence of novels is in the role of the woman, who takes on an increasingly positive importance. If we go back to *The Demon Lover*, Veronica Mainwaring is, to begin with, no more than a passive victim of Justin Lucas even if she becomes in the end, by her own decision, the vehicle for his redemption. In *The Winged Bull* Ursula is also in many respects a victim of male manipulation, arguably as much of Brangwyn's as of Hugo Astley and Frank Fouldes, although she ends up very much on equal terms with Ted. In *The Goat-foot God* however, Mona Freeman plays a much more positive role right from the start, whilst in *The Sea Priestess* Vivien Le Fay Morgan is definitely very much in charge, a process that is continued in the subsequent *Moon Magic* where she calls the shots in a relationship with a much more powerful and dynamic man.

There was a similar trend in the non-occult novels that she wrote. In *The Scarred Wrists* a downtrodden illegitimate waif Pat Stone rises from typist to viscountess by the process of reforming a lordly misunderstood paranoid schizophrenic. In *The Hunters of Humans* Ann Studley negotiates a delicate conflict of loyalties as her father, a serial poisoner, is brought to book by the detective to whom she is romantically attached. Whilst in *Beloved of Ishmael* Nina Barnett by her attitude and example reforms a renegade white man from his criminal career as gun runner and slave trader on the west coast of Africa.

However, without any esoteric dimension to them, these works remain no more than slightly idiosyncratic examples of circulating library fare of the mid nineteen thirties. Dion Fortune's importance as a novelist lies in her unique position in the esoteric field, with a first hand knowledge of the inner dynamics about which she was writing, and the ability to write evocatively about them. Her novels are in fact manuals containing descriptions of certain forms of magical practice, the reasons for working in this particular way, with descriptions of what it may feel like to be a protagonist in a magical working.

There is a certain sense of anticlimax with the sudden departure of the sea priestess two thirds of the way through the book as Wilfred sets about putting his life back together again. However this process is obviously an important one in Dion Fortune's mind as in large part it provides the whole point of the book, depicting the achievement of an ideal marriage from unpromising beginnings. This comes about by Wilfred and Molly putting into practice the principles of the sea priestess with the talismanic aid of the necklace of star sapphires.

By the end of the novel in fact, Molly has been transformed from a put upon mouse into a fulfilled and vital woman with conscious contacts with the Priest of the Moon, with a transformed Wilfred as her priest as well as her husband. It is not without significance that they have moved out of the small town atmosphere of Dickford to a farmhouse at the landward end of Bell Head. Thus if this evocative promontory into the Atlantic Ocean should be conceived as an ancient and magical place, rather than reverting to the old fort at the seaward end, at the mercy of the wild elements of storm and sea, where the sea priestess had performed her pioneering work with Wilfred, having formed a stable partnership, Molly and Wilfred can now develop their work at the productive landward end, where are now growing once again, as in days of yore, the Dionysian vines.

Although it is not described in detail, the climax of the book is once again a Rite of Isis, but performed by Molly rather than Vivien this time, with a significant difference that Molly invokes the god within her husband and priest: "Come unto me, Great Pan, come unto me!"

There follows a description by Wilfred of the depths of a human relationship that can be achieved between a man and a woman when both realise its cosmic extensions. Having passed out into another dimension their relationship has taken on a significance that is no longer merely personal but part of Life itself in the process of eternal becoming. Molly is to him not simply an individual woman, but all women. And in this realisation of the great principle of which she is an individual representative, life comes in with such a rush that they feel whirled away like leaves in the wind. The barriers of personality go down, they are made one with the cosmic life — not simply in the possession of each other, if indeed that is ever possible, or the desire for it not a false turning - but at one with a larger whole. Paradoxically, losing themselves in the larger life, they find each other.

Chapter Six

Moon Magic

The Story

Dr. Rupert Malcolm is a distinguished medical consultant, at the peak of his profession, but with a non-existent emotional, social or sexual life. His wife has become a resentful permanent invalid after a disastrous miscarriage of their first child, and their relationship, such as it is, is now no more than financial. As a consequence, despite his brilliance he is a tyrant to colleagues, students and patients alike.

His imagination has been haunted for many years by the recurring dream of a combined land and seascape in which a mysterious cloaked figure with a broad brimmed hat may appear. One foggy evening while walking along the Thames embankment he is intrigued to see a similar figure walking before him some twenty yards ahead, whom, despite the speed of his walking, he is unable to overtake. He loses track of her when she turns over Lambeth Bridge.

He begins to fantasise about this scene, playing it over and over again in his mind, and at the same time finds his attention drawn to a lighted window in an old church opposite his lodgings on the other side of the river. He also discovers that his dreaming about the cloaked figure seems dependent upon whether that light has been extinguished for the night. Some time later he comes again upon the figure walking before him along the Embankment. This time he follows her across the bridge, to discover that she lives in the converted church. He impulsively follows her through the door where she rebuffs him and he retires considerably embarrassed and crestfallen.

He continues to fantasise about her and finds his fantasy taking on an ever greater sense of reality, to the point of feeling that there is someone physically present but unseen. Finally, an unexpected person turns up at his consulting rooms, it is the mysterious woman whom he has previously been following.

She announces herself to be Miss Le Fay Morgan, says she has been troubled of late by a ghostly figure and produces a copy of the book *Phantasms of the Living*. He realises that his fantasising must have been the cause of this and abjectly says that he will no more indulge in the practice. On the contrary she invites him to collaborate with her in what she describes as a psychological experiment.

The story now continues in the words of Miss Le Fay Morgan. She is the same character we have met in *The Sea Priestess*, only she now uses the forename of Lilith, a name favoured by her father but banned by the vicar at her baptism. She recounts her work with Wilfred Maxwell and her coming to London, where she has found an old church in which to live and has equipped it with a magical temple. She also records her side of her recent experiences with Dr Rupert Malcolm, including some visionary research into a previous incarnation when they met in the temples of ancient Egypt.

Although she has described their possible work together in terms of a psychological experiment, it is not long before she reveals her magical intentions to Dr Malcolm. He, for his part, confesses his growing love for her only to be told that she intends to transmute that love into power. The type of power of which she speaks means nothing to him but she explains that three paths lie before them – to break off all contact altogether, to indulge in a full physical sexual relationship, or to keep their relationship on an entirely magical plane, with this last as the only one in which she is interested.

He agrees to her conditions and in a sequence of work in her magical temple she gradually introduces him to the conception of an invisible reality behind appearances, and instructs him in the aims of her magical work. This is intended to culminate in a Rite of Isis similar to that worked with Wilfred Maxwell, only now she has a considerably more vital and active partner.

She elaborates her ideas on the state of an ideal magical relationship, which whilst not lacking in mutual affection does not involve any notion of dependence upon or possessiveness toward the other. Physical sex she regards as no more than a fail-safe mechanism if the magical tensions should become too great and the power get out of control. In other words, if the relationship becomes physical then the magical work will have failed.

A crisis occurs when Malcolm's wife takes a turn for the worse and an urgent operation is required. This seems to be some kind of test for him, as he could easily have let her die, for the majority medical opinion is that her case is hopeless, and her death would have gained freedom for himself and at least the notional possibility of marriage to Lilith. Nonetheless he insists on trying to save his wife's life in an operation in which he personally assists, despite his deep aversion to the sight of blood. (His medical specialism is in nervous diseases, which do not require hands on surgical techniques, and we learn that his aversion to blood apparently stems from unfortunate events as a sacrificial priest in ancient Egypt.)

His return after this ordeal, and a realisation of its karmic implications, leads to Lilith performing a further stage in the Rite of Isis and a regular series of workings in which she prepares him for a major rite yet to come. Things are again brought to a temporary halt however by a sudden deterioration in his wife's condition, when she suffers a relapse and dies. Whilst this may seem a natural resolution of his karmic situation Lilith insists that his new found freedom makes no difference to the platonic status of their magical relationship.

This comes as a bitter disappointment to him but on completing their Isis work together he experiences heights of magical and mystical reality which he never knew existed, and comes to realise the truth and validity of all that she has been saying – not only as to the relationship between the sexes and its different modes of being but also the possibilities of high magical working.

*   *   *

Dion Fortune confessed to having some trouble in writing this book, until after half a dozen false starts she began to write it in the first person, from the viewpoint of Lilith Le Fay Morgan, when it started to flow. However, other concerns prevented her from finishing it. The exigencies of the 2nd World War with its disruption of routines, her involvement with various other esoteric ventures, and the curtailment of publishing due to paper rationing all no doubt played their part. It was finished by another hand, that of her friend and disciple Anne Fox, when it was posthumously published in 1956.

It thus falls naturally into three sections; the first three chapters, entitled *A Study in Telepathy* are presumably the best result of her early attempts at starting it; the central twelve chapters entitled *The Moon Mistress* written in the first person from the point of view of Lilith; and then the final three chapters, entitled *A Door Without A Key*, reverting to a third person account of Rupert Malcolm's experience of magical working and the culmination of their work together.

Dion Fortune found writing the middle section to be an educative experience insofar that the character took on a life of her own and expounded a great deal of very odd lore that Dion Fortune says she had not known anything about until she read it in her own pages. It is of course not unknown for characters apparently to take on a life of their own in the sphere of creative writing, and it sometimes results in very good writing and sometimes in very bad. In Dion Fortune's case, it has the added spice of a magical dimension, and she asked, only half in jest, if she had perhaps created a dark familiar for herself, as a number of her colleagues who read the manuscript also found the figure extremely evocative.

Dion Fortune concedes that the character might well represent her own Freudian subconsciousness, for there is a great deal in Lilith that she finds in herself, although on the other hand there is a great deal in Lilith that she does not. Lilith is entirely pagan, whereas Dion Fortune had a deep if somewhat unorthodox Christian commitment. Lilith is above all a rebel against society, bent upon its alteration, which she aims to effect by magical means.

The first part of the novel sets the scene for the magical involvement of Dr Rupert Malcolm with Lilith Le Fay Morgan. Its title, *A Study in Telepathy*, aptly describes its substance, at any rate to some degree, for besides being a study in telepathy it goes well beyond the projection of abstract thoughts from one person to another. This is after the lines of the body of evidence that is contained in the classic work by Gurney and Podmore *Phantasms of the Living*. However, it is not in experiments in telepathy or the projection of consciousness that the characters are ultimately concerned but in the dynamics of ritual magic.

There are other elements at work in the particularly strong relationship that develops between Lilith and Rupert, for if the reincarnationary record is to be believed they are by no means complete strangers. There are the forces of karma at work based upon events in a long distant priestly life in ancient Egypt.

Furthermore, Dr Malcolm is a man with a vivid pictorial imagination, and one accustomed to intense concentration, whilst Lilith, by way of her esoteric training, is more than usually psychically sensitive. It is thus perhaps no great wonder that she becomes aware of the fantasies that he is building up about her, particularly when events conspire to bring about more than one physical confrontation between the two, first when she nearly runs him down in her car, and the other upon the threshold of her house. After this she begins to reciprocate, bringing to him the awareness of an apparition of herself within his room, before taking the initiative upon the physical level and going to confront him at his consulting rooms. Here she invites him to a more conscious co-operation, allegedly as a psychological experiment, although with rather different motives than he can suspect at the time.

This brings us to the central part of the book, *The Moon Mistress*, recounted by Lilith herself. She begins with some rather startling assumptions. First that she may be 120 years old, which is a considerable advance even on that of *The Sea Priestess* when, although evidently much older than she appeared, she seemed likely to be no more than in her seventies. Of course we might well assume that in these claims she is carrying through her tactic of encouraging us to construct an image of her to concur with her own aspirations as a priestess of the goddess. 120 years is a symbolic number that has manifold associations in esoteric lore.

Another element in this personal mythology is the suggestion of an out of the ordinary kind of birth, suggesting she might have been some kind of changeling. This is a reflection from Dion Fortune's own life, for much the same story was told about her by her own mother, and she also evokes it in *The Sea Priestess*, although in connection with Wilfred Maxwell, as he speculates about the reasons for his being a misfit in local society.

As in *The Winged Bull* we have an element of significant ancestry, as Lilith traces her own back through dual Celtic lines of Welsh and Breton, not merely to exotic Pheonician origins, but to the possibilities of Atlantean colonialists upon the western seaboard of Europe. She also refers us back to *The*

Sea Priestess for an account of her introduction to the magical arts, encouraged by an older woman, using the devices of ouija and crystal ball, and also of course the details of her most recent magical work.

On arrival in London she has found a residence eminently suited to her requirements on the south bank of the Thames. The description of the building is based upon one that Dion Fortune used for the performance of her *Rite of Isis* in real life at much the same time as writing the novels. Known as The Belfry, its actual location is in West Halkin Street in Belgravia, somewhat north of the river, but for the purposes of the novel she has relocated it somewhere along what is nowadays the Albert Embankment. A converted church of early Victorian vintage, it takes on the lineaments of a desirable residence behind a deceptive façade (a favoured device of another of her adepts, Alick Brangwyn in *The Winged Bull*) where Lilith is loyally and idiosyncratically served by Mr Meatyard, one of Dion Fortune's more colourful minor characters, a rough diamond with great comic petty criminal and working class charm.

In this change of locale she considers that the days of her training have finished and that she is passing from the Lesser to the Greater Mysteries. This may also be indicated by her change of name from Vivien to Lilith although she also seems to favour being known as Le Fay. Along with this she confides her credo as to what being an adept is all about, citing the theme of the black coated adept with mysterious powers who appears from nowhere in response to some call for help and disappears equally mysteriously after that help has been given, as has been described in *Zanoni* by the mid 19th century novelist Edward Bulwer Lytton. She now proposes to tell the story from the adept's point of view.

In her belief she is the agent of a hierarchy upon the inner planes that is concerned with the inner governance of the world, not in terms of politics but in the spiritual influences that rule the minds of men. Some souls enter the world with the precise intention of cooperating with these powers, and such a one will have been prepared and trained for this task in previous lives.

She recalls Atlantean memories seeing herself as one who served in the courts of the great Sun temple in the City of the Golden Gates on the island of Ruta, and who was sent away before its catastrophic end to become one of the seed bearers for the next epoch. She also recalls a sequence of lives in the priesthood of ancient Egypt in the cult of the Black Isis – a frequently misunderstood side of the goddess - that is not evil but a reservoir of dynamic primordial force that, when it wells up, can break old forms so that new life may spring from them. She uses as an example her treatment of Wilfred Maxwell, whose old life she admits to breaking up, only for him to rise like a phoenix from the ashes of his former downtrodden existence. She obviously has much the same thing in mind with Rupert Malcolm whom she describes as a dour type encased in the plate armour of middle class convention and professional prestige.

Her wider purpose however is to return to the world as a priestess of the Great Goddess, as the old world breaks up in the cataclysmic period of world war, bringing with her the memory of forgotten arts at the dawn of a new aeon. She sees it her task to bring certain concepts to the subconscious mind of the race, and the way to do this is not by lecturing or writing, which addresses the conscious mind only, but by living the life with deliberate intention - to BE the Path as well as to tread it.

This, however, is not a thing that she can do single handedly. She needs to induce someone else to believe in her and the goddess within her, then the goddess can manifest.

We have seen the way she goes about this in her approach to Wilfred Maxwell and here she clearly states that she realises some people may sneer at her as a theatrical poseuse. Nonetheless she maintains that her theatre is a valid psychological one and her pose one that induces auto-suggestion in those for whom it is intended. In other of her works we know Dion Fortune to be well aware of the methods of Coué, through his disciple Baudouin's popular work of the 1920's *Suggestion and Autosuggestion*. However the type of suggestion that Lilith proposes is one that works with colour, movement, sound and light, not merely by the spoken word, working upon the imagination by means of the stage setting of her personal life, with the collection of symbolic artefacts from old temples, dim lighting to preserve their magnetism, aromatics such as sandal, cedar, camphor, musk, galbanum and frankincense, the essential oils of geranium, jasmine and attar, all suggestive of the great days of the past when the cult of Isis was at the height of its power, in the hope of awakening deeper memories within the selected few who come into her ambit.

Those with whom she seeks to work must, however, have certain qualities. Mere intellect is not enough, they must have something of the artist within them, and above all the curious gift of what she calls magnetism or vitality. This is certainly what Rupert Malcolm appears to have in abundance, albeit over-strained and embittered, and which was also present if not so readily apparent in Wilfred Maxwell until she stimulated it within him.

She also requires a suitable place in which to stage all this and describes acquiring and converting the old church in keeping with her tastes, which are as refined as those we have previously observed in the adept Alick Brangwyn in *The Winged Bull*.

She also evocatively describes the mystical contacts that are available from the river as she sits on a great bulk of timber on a wharf looking westward into the setting sun. Significantly, it is then that she notices the windows of the house across the river that are the lodgings of Rupert Malcolm. This induces speculations about the man she nearly ran down when she first drove into London, who of course happens to have been

Malcolm, by one of those coincidences that are not infrequent in the lives of initiates, and are not necessarily a convenient device for the popular novelist. Lilith intuitively divines his actual circumstances, of a man with a sex problem, living apart from his wife through no fault of his own, and yet barred by convention and inhibition from seeking an alternative to a natural and decent human outlet.

If his own wife will not live with him, she asks herself, why should he not live with somebody else's wife whose husband would not live with her, and have a new deal all round? But such a simple solution is bedevilled by the property values attached to the marriage laws and the moral values attached to virginity. This was a problem that much exercised Dion Fortune at this time and indeed much of contemporary society. She fulsomely praised a play by Charles Morgan that ran on the West End stage at this time, *The Flashing Stream*. It caused something of a furore through advocating that there is nothing wrong with a physical sexual relationship if no-one else is harmed by it. Morgan, dramatic critic on *The Times*, went on to write a book to justify his position, which was of course shared by many, at least in more liberal circles of society.

By further happy coincidence Lilith has discovered a concealed octagonal room at the top of the house that admirably suits her purposes as a temple, and is not unconscious of the irony that it seems originally to have served as the illicit love nest for a previous incumbent of the church, who in the novel seems to have been something of a maverick.

She describes her furnishing of this temple in some detail. This is minimal, at any rate by magical standards. Walls and carpeted floor are black, with a cubical altar in the centre of the octogon over which hangs a bronze lamp bearing a Perpetual Light of the spirit. Upon each of the seven walls, apart from the western one that contains the door and represents Earth, is the sigil of one of the traditional planets, (Saturn, Jupiter, Mars, Sol, Venus, Mercury). The eastern side opposite the door represents the Moon, and is graced with a long mirror over which is a symbol of the horned moon. (If she were working with any of the other planetary potencies then that would be the one located in the east, with its symbol over the mirror, she later explains. At the present however she is working exclusively with the Moon.)

Between the mirror and the altar is a pastos, or narrow black couch, upon each side of which stands a pillar, one black and the other silver. Upon the altar are the four symbolic weapons of the Elements, wand, cup, dagger, pentacle. It is a very simple arrangement with no colours but black and silver, and, as she pointedly remarks, without all the symbolic trappings that are needed to impress those who are not aware of what real magical work is all about.

She lists out the requirements for preparing such a temple for magical work. It must be a place concealed and set apart so that no outsiders can contaminate it with their thoughts, it must contain the symbols relevant to the specific work in hand and nothing else, and most importantly it must have an astral counterpart built over it — that is to say strongly visualised with the imagination of a trained mind. She then describes the astral overlay she intends to use, building it up with the help of a suitably trained friend. This is slightly more elaborate than the physical counterpart and incorporates a Composition of Mood by means of treading an imaginary journey.

They picture a great ancient Egyptian temple of Isis, first in broad outline and then in detail. Each in turn describes what she sees in imagination so that there is a mutual agreement and coordination in the building. By these means they approach the temple along an avenue of ram headed sphinxes that leads to a pylon gate in the temenos wall. Beyond this is a court containing a lotus pool, and shadowed colonnades leading to the bronze doors that give on to a great hall of pillars. As they do this, alternately describing and watching, the fantasised scenes begin to take on a feeling of reality as they no longer observe them with the mind's eye but feel themselves actually walking about within the scene. The general plan is like an ankh, with the lotus pool as the vertical bar, the hall (which is elsewhere called the Hall of Sphinxes) the horizontal bar, with the holy of holies behind the curtain in an ovoid space. Within the great hall is a circle of the zodiac inset in the marble floor and above it the perpetual light that shines in every Mystery temple, and at the far end the raised seats for the priests beyond which a heavy curtain conceals the holy of holies.

There is also, in a recess beside this curtain, an arch that leads down a sloping passageway to a temple in the distant hills – a pre-dynastic temple older even than the Egyptian civilisation. It contains a great black basalt statue of the goddess with the negroid features of the black Hamitic people of ancient time, a table for human sacrifice before her. This temple has fallen into disuse apart from a tradition as to its existence with its entrance said to be lost in the desert sands. However, this passage to it is still known to the higher priesthood, aware that the ancient temple represents the origins of their own more civilised rites, and they still use it for higher initiations that are known only to a few.

The great hall itself appears to be empty but it contains the astral form of a mummified figure of Isis lying in a sarcophagus, and like a vision within a vision this figure begins to become visible to the two builders who have now visualised themselves to be seated in the seats of the priests. This part of the work having been completed they agree to proceed through to what they call the Black Temple, but as they do so they become aware that another is with them. It is a sacrificial priest, who by his function is perfectly entitled to be there, but such priests were grim and sinister figures who were given this role as a means of expiating some serious crime. They were shunned by the rest of the priesthood despite their relatively high standing within the hierarchy.

This unwelcome addition to their visualisation marks the end of this initial piece of magical working by Lilith and her friend, for it appears that it is not simply a memory of ancient time but is an actual present time interference from some unknown source, despite the strength of their astral sealing and lack of break in concentration.

With the mystery unsolved, that night Lilith has a vivid dream of walking by the sea pursued by a stranger. Soon after she becomes aware of being followed along the embankment one evening when on her way home. Indeed we are now treated to Lilith's perspective upon the events that have been previously described. Rupert Malcolm's persistent fantasising about her has caused him to impinge even upon her temple meditations. She decides to take a more positive role in all of this by means of astral projection, the process of which she describes. She pictures herself standing six feet in front of herself and then transfers consciousness to this simulacrum so as to look at the room through its eyes. Then she visualises Rupert's face (whom she has already met and made eye contact with, which she finds to be an important factor in making magic real) and imagines herself speaking to him. This imaginative device brings about an immediate change of consciousness as she finds herself aware of being in his physical presence, looking around his rooms, upon the astral plane. She sees him in a condition of great emotional turmoil, and in compassion, as he drifts off to sleep and into a condition of psychic receptivity, she draws off some of the seething vitality that whirls about him. Then she returns to her temple where she offers up the power she has absorbed to the figure of Isis which she visualises standing behind her reflected in the mirror.

She confesses that the process has been somewhat after the nature of being a succubus or even a vampire, but that in this instance the act and the motivation are entirely beneficial – which is indeed a long way from the abuse of the technique we have seen on the part of Justin Lucas in *The Demon Lover*.

It is immediately following this that she decides that the time has come to take the initiative physically, and beard him in his consulting rooms, for he will never come to her through his own accord, after the previous embarrassment of being turned away at her door.

All this has been the culmination of some period of waiting, and of what she describes as a little realised aspect of esoteric work, the discernment of patterns in life which indicate that intelligent inner forces are at work. Such patterns are generally discerned as a recurring event or image. In this case it is the series of coincidences in which the same man has figured. It commenced with her almost running him down in her car when she first arrived in London, then becoming aware of his house across the water, and finally of him following her. In all this we also see a certain vulnerability in the priestess, conscious of the possible threat of physical assault by an unknown stalker, and even her astral venture has problems inherent with projecting across water, which is a great absorber of astral energies, hence its traditional safeguard as a barrier against witches.

We have now been provided with the background to their meeting and can proceed to the story of how she trains him to assist her magical work. However, for the time being there is nothing to be done but to wait until he actively responds to her invitation to work with her on what she has described as a psychological experiment.

There are considerable barriers of inhibition and convention that prevent Dr Malcolm from approaching her readily again, but she is aware that his thoughts continue to centre upon her. This includes a powerful experience, which she recounts as being a curious study in telepathy. Sitting in the darkness of her room, lit only by the firelight and the concentrated beam from a reading lamp by which she is sewing one of her robes, her attention is drawn to the flash of the stones of two rings she is wearing, a black pearl and a black diamond which put her in mind of the polar interchange of the goddesses Isis and

Nephthys. She then becomes aware of the face of Malcolm, so vividly as almost to appear like a materialisation before her. She realises it to be more than mere imagination however by the vitality of the eyes, which appear alive and to have the soul of the man looking through them. This, it would appear, is some kind of spontaneous astral projection on his part, perhaps aided by his perusal of the book she had left with him, *Phantasms of the Living*.

Nonetheless still no word comes from him, but she begins to become used to the projection of his thoughts in her direction, whether sitting on her own or about her daily life out and about in town. Then, one evening when she is performing her usual meditation prior to going to sleep, which consists of going down a long avenue of cypresses towards a temple dedicated to Isis, she finds him following her in her vision. She stops and takes his hand and they enter the temple together to stand beneath the perpetual light in the centre of the zodiacal mosaic pavement although she takes care to ensure that the curtain is kept drawn before the inner sanctum. Slowly and deliberately she repeats to him, in case his psychism is not readily up to receiving the communication easily, that he is welcome to come here to worship at any time. Then she passes on through the black curtain into the inner sanctum which no one but she can enter.

When she returns he is still present. Taking his hand she leads him back out through the lotus court and down the long avenue where they part, he to cross the river and return to earth life and she to pass on to her inner abode for the night, which she refers to as the House of the Virgins. This situation goes on for some time, and it would also appear that Lilith is engaged in occult work with others as well, for she notes that some of them also sense his presence, with varying reactions.

Events come to a climax soon after the Winter Solstice when her evening visualisation has passed over into dream, as, she says, it should in one well practised in it. She finds herself standing with him under the perpetual light only to be rudely disturbed and awoken by the feeling of someone gripping her upper arms. She wakes, and finds nobody there, but someone or something has seized her strongly enough to cause serious bruising. This gives her pause for thought. It suggests that Rupert's projection has become so strong, even if it be across water, as to become almost a complete materialisation. However, nothing further happens. It seems as if the incident, however it may have appeared to him, has scared Rupert Malcolm too and he has ceased any further work of this nature. She no longer feels any magnetic flow between them, and realises how badly she misses it.

So things proceed until the Vernal Equinox, a time of swirling astral currents when the inner tides change. In the calm waters that ensue this crisis point she is once again aware of him, although in a much weaker state than heretofore. She comes to the conclusion that following the Winter Solstice crisis some other party has been arbitrarily intervening. She decides that she will have to do something about this, and going to her temple she seals it with astral pentagrams at the four quarters and clad in her black robe and silver head dress invokes the lion headed goddess Sekhmet. Feeling the lioness head forming over her own on the astral ethers, she draws a magic circle about herself and a triangle of evocation into which she evokes the presence of Rupert Malcolm. Then encircling them both with a ring of fire she commands that none shall in future come between them in their work of Isis.

Although the actual work takes no more than half an hour, such is the power involved that it takes a couple of days to recover from the strain of it. She receives confirmation of its success when a friend contacts her to report a vivid dream in which she was told to pass on an instruction from the Priest of the Moon to tell Lilith that she must "give the message". Such confirmation, Lilith says, is always forthcoming when serious work is afoot. Events then take a turn of their own when, shortly afterwards, she meets Dr Malcolm, apparently by chance, on the riverfront close by.

He says that he has been meaning to visit her and announces that he wants to co-operate fully with whatever she may have in mind. She then begins the slow process of explaining magic to this eminent man of science.

It becomes apparent what has been causing the rift in their previous inter-relationship. He, worried that his fantasising might be getting out of hand, had gone to a psychoanalyst who after some unsuccessful attempts at hypnotic suggestion had passed him on to a New Thought practitioner. This had also seemed likely to prove abortive, until the point came when he distinctly felt Lilith's inner call to him. This would have been when she performed her invocation, banishing all who tried to come between them.

In the course of their exchange of information he tells how he has had a recurring nightmare since childhood of being locked in a room alone with the task of having to dissect a woman and knowing that when he has done so he will be killed. In his mind he is now convinced that the woman concerned was Lilith, which seems confirmed when he recognises her from a plate in a reference book on mummies. This goes some way to persuade him that the dream might relate to a previous life, perhaps in ancient Egypt, whose religion is the only one that has ever had any appeal for him.

Lilith encourages him in this belief and starts the long process of introducing him to the work she has in mind. She is in the extremely unusual situation of trying to instruct a complete neophyte in advanced magical working, and moreover one who has a scientific and medical background. It is a task whose magnitude and difficulty she compares with a labour of Hercules.

The first steps are hardly promising.

"Do you believe in life after death?" - "No."

Nor does he see any reason to believe in the existence of

an ancient secret wisdom, but as he has never looked for one, neither is he prepared categorically to deny it. But if there is any such, from his experience of her to date he is quite prepared to believe that Lilith has it. He also concedes that she seems to have certain unusual powers, and if she says that this is a result of such ancient wisdom then perhaps he would do well to believe her.

Gradually Lilith leads him to the view that there can be a two way cause and effect between mind and matter, for it is mind that produces matter in the first place, that all springs from the spiritual and mental worlds, and that mind and spirit are not simply an emanation of the body – even if once the mould has been made in a bodily sense, it cannot be readily altered by spirit or mind.

She cites the theories of autohypnosis and deliberately induced dissociation of personality as being part of the method of the Mysteries, which he is inclined to regard as nothing more than artificially induced and localised insanity – the cultivation of hyper-suggestibility. She replies that it may well seem to start like that, but there is definitely something more as she will prove to him in the course of the work they have undertaken. That the next stage is access to the higher levels of consciousness, beyond the subconscious mind.

He admits to being able to get a glimmer of what she is driving at, and can see how a psychological aspect comes into it that is quite reasoned, just as he can see the physiological aspect of the central nervous system in the operations of yoga. He has so far not seen anything in her work that could not be explained psychologically, but he can see she understands the psychological basis. He agrees to continue to work with her and to keep a meticulous record of his experiences.

Thus the work continues, with Lilith homing in on the natural cleavage in his personality, which is the fundamental problem with his marriage, which would appear to be of karmic origin, and the vivid nightmares which suggest the origin in terms of moral trauma in a past life.

In what to a certain degree is a form of psychoanalysis using her own methods, Rupert Malcolm's dream develops into a vision of having in ancient time conceived a lust for a priestess of the Egyptian Mysteries, whom he now identifies as Lilith, to have murdered a priest and taken his place in the temple in order to violate the priestess, for which blasphemous crime he was subsequently painfully put to death. The karmic element is to be found in the frustrations of his present marriage and the way that his hospital work is every bit as constricting as he found his expiatory work as a sacrificial priest in ancient Egypt. The problems of the present are rooted in the past, but their appearance as problems in this life means they have come up for resolution. It is this that has led the two of them together, so that he may now redeem himself and express in proper magical terms what he abused and violated in the past.

In tandem with these realisations Rupert Malcolm is gradually introduced to Lilith's temple and to the principles of ritual working. In the earlier stages Lilith has to provide the driving force by her own will power until such time as she can work him up to an emotional pitch where he begins to draw from deeper reserves of energy and wisdom that will overcome his inhibitions and prejudices and contribute magnetism of his own to the work. As the pressure of the inner forces begins to overcome his ingrained and natural scepticism, she has to deftly handle the process and hold him steady so that he does not over-react and lose control.

Thus we have a series of sessions in the temple where he is largely the recipient of her evocations of aspects of the goddess, or the divine feminine principle, which in orthodox christianity is limited to the heavenly ideal of the Blessed Virgin Mary, if at all, but which Lilith approaches via various pagan goddess forms and in particular those of Persephone, Isis and Aphrodite.

The final part of the novel, *The Door without a Key*, reverts to third person narrative to show how Lilith's ministrations have had a major effect upon Rupert Malcolm's personal and professional life. He is now on far better terms of relationship with colleagues, patients and students, and we see him demonstrating the existence of the etheric double in a case of "glove and stocking" anaesthesia and seriously discussing *Phantasms of the Living* with one of his students.

All this is but a preliminary to a full performance of the Rite of Isis as experienced by Rupert Malcolm when he crosses the bar that separates normal personality consciousness from higher consciousness. He becomes aware of himself and Lilith as they really are as spiritual beings, their souls, no longer two circles bounded by their peripheries, but two centres of radiation whose rays meet and mingle, and that a gateway has been opened for him on the threshold to a greater world. He has been vouchsafed the means to approach and to pass through "the Door without a Key".

Index

A Rebours, 77
Assegioli, 82
Astral Body, The, 47
Atlantis, 45, 60, 105, 110, 125
Avalon, Arthur, 47
Avebury, 83
Axbridge, 109

Belfry, The, 124
Beloved of Ishmael, The, 107, 115
Blavatsky, 39, 78
Brean Down, 109
Brent Knoll, 109
British Museum, 53, 57
Bromage, Bernard, 90, 114

Carrington, Hereward, 47, 103
Causal Body, The, 47
Chalice Orchard, 65
Circuit of Force, The, 46, 70
Corn King and the Spring Queen, The, 73, 77, 78, 98
Crowley, Aleister, 80, 113

Devil's Mistress, The, 73, 77
Dion Fortune and the Inner Light, 40

Eleusis, 44, 89, 96
Eranos Foundation/Institute, 48, 90
Esoteric Orders and their Work, The, 38
Etheric Double, The, 47
Euripides, 78
Evans, Thomas Penry, 11, 91

Flashing Stream, The, 127
Fornario, Netta, 40
Freud, 78, 97
Frobe-Kapteyn, Olga, 48

Glastonbury Tor, 84
Golden Dawn, Hermetic Order of, 36, 48, 77, 82
Guild of the Master Jesus, 64
Gurney & Podmore, 122

Hegel, 78
Hinton, 78
Human Aura, The, 47
Hunters of Humans, 107, 115
Huysman, 73, 77

Iamblichos, 78, 79
Inner Light Magazine, 29, 46, 67, 70, 108
Innes, Brodie, 73, 77, 79, 80
Instincts of the Herd in Peace and War, 68
Introduction to Ritual Magic, An, 42
Iona, 40
Ireland, 112

Jung, 94
Jungle Book, The, 27

Kilner, 47
Kipling, 27
Knights Templar, 88

La Bas, 73, 77
Lindisfarne, 72, 83
Literature of Illuminism, The, 47

Loveday, C. T., 64
Lytton, Edward Bulwer, 124

Maeterlinck, 78
Magick, 80
Mahatma Letters, 39
Mason, A. E. W., 73, 77
Medico-Psychological Clinic, 12
Mitcheson, Naomi, 73, 77, 78, 79
Mont St. Michel, 84
Moonchild, 113
Morgan, Charles, 127
Moriarty, Theodore, 12-14, 39
Muldoon, Sylvan, 47, 48, 113
Mystical Meditations on the Collects, 64
Mystical Qabalah, The, 57, 64, 107

Novalis, 78

Occult Review, The, 17, 37

Petronius, 79
Powell, A. E., 47
Phantasms of the Living, 119, 122, 132, 137
Practical Occultism, 47
Principles of Esoteric Healing, 11, 87
Principles of Tantra, 47
Prisoner in the Opal, The, 73, 77, 79
Projection of the Astral Body, The, 47, 103
Psychic Self-Defence, 39, 40, 41

Rakoczi, Master, 37
Rite of Isis, 113
Royal Magazine, 11

Sane Occultism, 18, 37
Scarred Wrists, The, 107, 115
Secret of the Golden Flower, The, 94
Serpent Power, The, 47
Societas Rosicruciana in Anglia, 36
Solomon, Temple of, 112
Spencer, Herbert, 79
Spiritual Exercises of St. Ignatius Loyola, 77, 80, 94
Spiritualism and Occultism, 40
St. Albans, 83
St. Alban's (Alden's) Head, 72, 83
St. Augustine, 88
Steele, V. M., 107
St. Francis, 88, 89
St. Ignatius of Loyola, 77, 80, 94
St. Michael's Mount, 84
St. Monica, 88
Suggestion and Auto-Suggestion, 47, 126
Swinburne, 55

Theosophical Society, 64
Thorley, 84
Tintagel, 83
Training and Work of an Initiate, The, 38
Trotter, Wilfred, 68

Watson, William, 55
West Halkin Street, 124
Weston-super-Mare, 109
What is Occultism? 18, 37
Woodroffe, Sir John, 47
Zanoni, 124

Other titles from Thoth Publications

THE CIRCUIT OF FORCE

by Dion Fortune.
With commentaries by Gareth Knight.

In "The Circuit of Force", Dion Fortune describes techniques for raising the personal magnetic forces within the human aura and their control and direction in magic and in life, which she regards as 'the Lost Secrets of the Western Esoteric Tradition'.

To recover these secrets she turns to three sources.

a) the Eastern Tradition of Hatha Yoga and Tantra and their teaching on raising the "sleeping serpent power" or kundalini;

b) the circle working by means of which spiritualist seances concentrate power for the manifestation of some of their results;

c) the linking up of cosmic and earth energies by means of the structured symbol patterns of the Qabalistic Tree of Life.

Originally produced for the instruction of members of her group, this is the first time that this material has been published for the general public in volume form.

Gareth Knight provides subject commentaries on various aspects of the etheric vehicle, filling in some of the practical details and implications that she left unsaid in the more secretive esoteric climate of the times in which she wrote.

Some quotes from Dion Fortune's text:

"When, in order to concentrate exclusively on God, we cut ourselves off from nature, we destroy our own roots. There must be in us a circuit between heaven and earth, not a one-way flow, draining us of all vitality. It is not enough that we draw up the Kundalini from the base of the spine; we must also draw down the divine light through the Thousand-Petalled Lotus. Equally, it is not enough for our mental health and spiritual development that we draw down the Divine Light, we must also draw up the earth forces. Only too often mental health is sacrificed to spiritual development through ignorance of, or denial of, this fact."

"....the clue to all these Mysteries is to be sought in the Tree of Life. Understand the significance of the Tree; arrange the symbols you are working with in the correct manner upon it, and all is clear and you can work out your sum. Equate the Danda with the Central Pillar, and the Lotuses with the Sephiroth and the bi-sections of the Paths thereon, and you have the necessary bilingual dictionary at your disposal - if you know how to use it."

ISBN 978-1-870450-28-7

SPIRITUALISM AND OCCULTISM
By Dion Fortune *with commentary edited by* Gareth Knight

As well as being an occultist of the first rank, Dion Fortune was an accomplished medium. Thus she is able to explain the methods, technicalities and practical problems of trance mediumship from first hand experience. She describes exactly what it feels like to go into trance and the different types of being one may meet with beyond the usual spirit guides.

For most of her life her mediumistic abilities were known only to her immediate circle until, in the war years, she responded to the call to try to make a united front of occultists and spiritualists against the forces of materialism in the post-war world. At this point she wrote various articles for the spiritualist press and appeared as a speaker on several spiritualist platforms

This book contains her original work *Spiritualism in the Light of Occult Science* with commentaries by Gareth Knight that quote extensively from now largely unobtainable material that she wrote on the subject during her life, including transcripts from her own trance work and rare articles from old magazines and journals.

This book represents the fourth collaborative work between the two, *An Introduction to Ritual Magic*, *The Circuit of Force*, and *Principles of Hermetic Philosophy* being already published in this series.

ISBN 978-1-870450-38-6

DION FORTUNE AND THE INNER LIGHT
By Gareth Knight

At last – a comprehensive biography of Dion Fortune based upon the archives of the Society of the Inner Light. As a result much comes to light that has never before been revealed. This includes: Her early experiments in trance mediumship with her Golden Dawn teacher Maiya Curtis-Webb and in Glastonbury with Frederick Bligh Bond, famous for his psychic investigations of Glastonbury Abbey.

The circumstances of her first contact with the Masters and reception of "The Cosmic Doctrine". The ambitious plans of the Master of Medicine and the projected esoteric clinic with her husband in the role of Dr. Taverner.

The inside story of the confrontation between the Christian Mystic Lodge of the Theosophical Society of which she was president, and Bishop Piggot of the Liberal Catholic church, over the Star in the East movement and Krishnamurti. Also her group's experience of the magical conflict with Moina MacGregor Mathers.

How she and her husband befriended the young Israel Regardie, were present at his initiation into the Hermes Temple of the Stella Matutina, and suffered a second ejection from the Golden Dawn on his subsequent falling out with it.

Her renewed and highly secret contact with her old Golden Dawn teacher Maiya Tranchell-Hayes and their development of the esoteric side of the Arthurian legends.

Her peculiar and hitherto unknown work in policing the occult jurisdiction of the Master for whom she worked which brought her into unlikely contact with occultists such as Aleister Crowley.

Nor does the remarkable story end with her physical death for, through the mediumship of Margaret Lumley Brown and others, continued contacts with Dion Fortune have been reported over subsequent years.

ISBN 978-1-870450-45-4

PRINCIPLES OF HERMETIC PHILOSOPHY
By Dion Fortune & Gareth Knight

Principles of Hermetic Philosophy was the last known work written by Dion Fortune. It appeared in her Monthly letters to members and associates of the Society of the Inner Light between November 1942 and March 1944.

Her intention in this work is summed up in her own words: "The observations in these pages are an attempt to gather together the fragments of a forgotten wisdom and explain and expand them in the light of personal observation."

She was uniquely equipped to make highly significant personal observations in these matters as one of the leading practical occultists of her time. What is more, in these later works she feels less constrained by traditions of occult secrecy and takes an altogether more practical approach than in her earlier, well known textbooks.

Gareth Knight takes the opportunity to amplify her explanations and practical exercises with a series of full page illustrations, and provides a commentary on her work

ISBN 978-1-870450-34-8

*   *   *   *   *

THE STORY OF DION FORTUNE
As told to Charles Fielding *and* Carr Collins.

Dion Fortune and Aleister Crowley stand as the twentieth century's most influential leaders of the Western Esoteric Tradition. They were very different in their backgrounds, scholarship and style.

But, for many, Dion Fortune is the chosen exemplar of the Tradition - with no drugs, no homosexuality and no kinks. This book tells of her formative years and of her development.

At the end, she remains a complex and enigmatic figure, who can only be understood in the light of the system she evolved and worked to great effect.

There can be no definitive "Story of Dion Fortune". This book must remain incomplete. However, readers may find themselves led into an experience of initiation as envisaged by this fearless and dedicated woman.

ISBN 978-1-879450-33-1

PRACTICAL OCCULTISM
By Dion Fortune *supplemented by* Gareth Knight

This book contains the complete text of Dion Fortune's *Practical Occultism in Dialy Life* which she wrote to explain, simply and practically, enough of the occult doctrines and methods to enable any reasonably intelligent and well balanced person to make practical use of them in the circumstances of daily life. She gives sound advice on remembering past incarnations, working out karma, divination, the use and abuse of mind power and much more.

Gareth Knight has delved into the Dion Fortune archive to provide additional material not available before outside Dion Fortune's immediate circle. It includes instruction on astral magic, the discipline of the mysteries, inner plane communicators, black magic and mental trespassing, nature contracts and elemental shrines.

In addition, Dion Fortune's review of *The Literature of Illuminism* describes the books she found most useful in her own quest, ranging from books for beginners to those on initiation, Qabalah, occult fiction, the old gods of England, Atlantis, witchcraft and yoga. In conclusion there is an interpretation by Dion Fortune's close friend Netta Fornario of *The Immortal Hour*, that haunting work of faery magic by Fiona Macleod, first performed at Glastonbury.

ISBN 978-1-870450-47-8

PRINCIPLES OF ESOTERIC HEALING
By Dion Fortune. *Edited and arranged by* Gareth Knight

One of the early ambitions of Dion Fortune along with her husband Dr Thomas Penry Evans was to found a clinic devoted to esoteric medicine, along the lines that she had fictionally described in her series of short stories *The Secrets of Dr. Taverner*. The original Dr. Taverner was her first occult teacher Dr. Theodore Moriarty, about whom she later wrote: "if there had been no Dr. Taverner there would have been no Dion Fortune!"

Shortly after their marriage in 1927 she and Dr. Evans began to receive a series of inner communications from a contact whom they referred to as the Master of Medicine. Owing to the pressure of all their other work in founding an occult school the clinic never came to fruition as first intended, but a mass of material was gathered in the course of their little publicised healing work, which combined esoteric knowledge and practice with professional medical expertise.

Most of this material has since been recovered from scattered files and reveals a fascinating approach to esoteric healing, taking into account the whole human being. Health problems are examined in terms of their physical, etheric, astral, mental or spiritual origination, along with principles of esoteric diagnosis based upon the structure of the Qabalistic Tree of Life. The function and malfunction of the psychic centres are described along with principles for their treatment by conventional or alternative therapeutic methods, with particular attention paid to the aura and the etheric double. Apart from its application to the healing arts much of the material is of wider interest for it demonstrates techniques for general development of the psychic and intuitive faculties apart from their more specialised use in assisting diagnosis.

ISBN 978-1-870450-85-0

PYTHONESS The Life & Work of Margaret Lumley Brown
By Gareth Knight

Margaret Lumley Brown was a leading member of Dion Fortune's Society of the Inner Light, taking over many of Dion Fortune's functions after the latter's death in 1946. She raised the arts of seership to an entirely new level and has been hailed with some justification as the finest medium and psychic of the 20th century. Although she generally sought anonymity in her lifetime her work was the source of much of the inner teachings of the Society from 1946 to 1961 and provided much of the material for Gareth Knight's *The Secret Tradition in Arthurian Legend* and *A Practical Guide to Qabalistic Symbolism*.

Gathered here is a four part record of the life and work of this remarkable woman. Part One presents the main biographical details largely as revealed by herself in an early work *Both Sides of the Door* an account of the frightening way in which her natural psychism developed as a consequence of experimenting with an ouija board in a haunted house. Part Two consists of articles written by her on such subjects as Dreams, Elementals, the Faery Kingdom, Healing and Atlantis, most of them commissioned for the legendary but short lived magazine *New Dimensions*. Part Three provides examples of her mediumship as Archpythoness of her occult fraternity with trance addresses on topics as diverse as Elemental Contacts, Angels and Archangels, Greek and Egyptian gods, and the Holy Grail. Part Four is devoted to the occult side of poetry, with some examples of her own work which was widely published in her day.

Gareth Knight was a colleague and friend of Margaret Lumley Brown in their days in the Society of the Inner Light together, to whom in later years she vouchsafed her literary remains, some esoteric memorabilia, and the privilege of being her literary executor.

ISBN 978-1-670450-75-1

MAGICAL KABBALAH
By Alan Richardson

The *Magical Kabbalah* is a revised and expanded re-release of an *Introduction to the Mystical Qabalah* which was written when the author was a teenager, has never been out of print in 30 years, and is regarded by some as the clearest, simplest, and most effective book on the topic ever written.

This excellent introduction presents a spiritual system that anyone can use to enhance his or her life. The reader learns how the Kabbalah can and should be self-taught, without joining expensive groups and paying for dodgy teachers with dubious motives. Whatever your spiritual path these tried and tested methods will expand your consciousness and broaden your grasp of the Western Esoteric Traditions as they exist today. They will also show how each person can help expand these traditions and become self-initiated in safe and potent ways.

Explore both the theories and principles behind ritual practice. Explore the ways in which the Kabbalah - the Tree of Life - can apply to (and make sense of) every aspect of everyday life. Perform astral magic, use the Tarot for self-exploration, energise ancient myths to make them come alive, revisit past lives, build patterns in your aura, work with the imagery of Egyptian and Arthurian magic, banish unpleasant atmospheres and create gates into other dimensions.

ISBN 978-1-870450-53-9